Six Miles to Charleston

SIX MILES

to

Charleston

THE TRUE STORY OF
JOHN AND LAVINIA FISHER

BRUCE ORR

THE
History
PRESS

Published by The History Press
Charleston, SC 29403
www.historypress.net

Front cover image: The Hanging of Lavinia Fisher *by David Gobel.*

First published 2010
Second printing 2012
Third printing 2012
Fourth printing 2012

ISBN 978.1.54020.533.9

Orr, Bruce.
Six miles to Charleston : the true story of John and Lavinia Fisher / Bruce Orr.
p. cm.
Includes bibliographical references.
ISBN 978-1-54020-533-9
1. Fisher, John, d. 1820. 2. Fisher, Lavinia, d. 1820. 3. Murderers--South Carolina--
Charleston--Biography. 4. Hotelkeepers--South Carolina--Charleston--Biography. 5.
Charleston (S.C.)--Biography. 6. Six Mile House (Charleston, S.C.)--History. 7. Charleston
(S.C.)--History--19th century. 8. Criminal justice, Administration of--South Carolina-
-Charleston--History--19th century. 9. Trials (Murder)--South Carolina--Charleston--
History--19th century. 10. Charleston (S.C.)--Politics and government--19th century. I.
Title.
HV6248.F47O7 2010
364.152'30922757915--dc22
2010041014

For my children: I have always taught you to search for the facts in the face of what others may tell you.
Rachel S.: Thank you for putting up with me after I have dragged you through the streets of Charleston in the rain, for tolerating me again after I dragged you through the dust and the dirt of the Old City Jail and also burying you in photos, files and microfiche.
"Catt Vee": My fantastic friend from Raleigh, I always told you that the first one's for you.

CONTENTS

FOREWORD

Many years ago after graduating from the Citadel Military College in Charleston, I, like many young men and women, was still trying to find my direction in life. All that changed with a single carriage tour through Charleston. That one trip was the beginning of a love affair with history, and it was also the beginning of Bulldog Tours.

When I began giving tours in 1991, ghost tours were only popular around Halloween. Ten years later, in the summer of 2001, while riding my bike home, I passed a ghost tour standing in front of a cemetery and was shocked that people would do such a tour, even in the heat of the summer. Two blocks later on that bike ride home, I randomly glanced down Broad Street to pay my respects to the Old Exchange, one of Charleston's crown jewels of historical buildings. It was at that point I had a life-changing epiphany that the dungeon at the bottom of the Old Exchange would be a phenomenal place to take a ghost tour. The "Ghost & Dungeon Walking Tour" started that fall and became an instant hit, especially after the filming of the Travel Channel's "America's Most Haunted Places." Our "Haunted Jail Tour" at the Old City Jail and the "Ghost & Graveyard Tour" at the Circular Congregational Church followed in the next few years. This was the formula for Bulldog Tours' initial success—taking visitors to historical and haunted locations.

As I approached each of the potential ghost-tour locations, I would not only receive valuable information as to the historical facts of that particular location, I would also hear tales of ghosts and numerous unexplainable events. The history of the buildings and the ghost stories were so often intertwined that it was impossible to separate them. They say every building in Charleston has its own story, and I say that is an understatement. Generations after generations have filled these buildings with numerous tales. Each building is not a single story; each building is a library within itself.

There is no better example of this than the Old City Jail.

Built in 1802 and used until 1939, thousands of people were housed there and thousands more died there. The Fishers were two such people.

The legend I heard as a child was that John and Lavinia Fisher ran the Six Mile House, a boardinghouse on the outskirts of Charleston in the early 1800s. They would rob and murder their guests as they slept. Some versions of the tale have Lavinia sedating or even killing the guests with the poisonous oleander flower that she mixed into a hot tea. John would then butcher the bodies and dispose of them in a cellar under the inn.

In early 1819, one of their victims managed to escape and flee back to Charleston where he alerted the authorities. The next morning the sheriff of Charleston, accompanied by many others, rode out to the Six Mile House and arrested the Fishers. While searching the property, the sheriff opened the cellar and made a gruesome discovery. The cellar contained the decomposing remains of numerous victims of the Fishers. Legend estimates thirty or more victims were found, but the butchering made the exact body count impossible to obtain.

In 1820, the Fishers were condemned to execution. Lavinia was convinced that she would be pardoned by the governor, and that he would not execute a woman. Her beauty and charm had saved her more than once, and she was sure it would save her now. She also requested to be hanged in her wedding gown to invoke sympathy from the large crowd gathered to witness the execution. She was said to be a very beautiful woman, and the image of a young woman in her wedding gown on the gallows would begin to burn in the minds of all those who witnessed the events as they were unfolding.

As a pastor attempted to lead Lavinia in repentance for her sins, she stopped him. She responded to his efforts by saying, "Cease! I will have none of it. Save your words for others that want them. But if you have a message you want to send to Hell, give it to me; I'll carry it."

And with that she leapt from the platform, hanging herself and denying the hangman the opportunity of executing her. Lavinia Fisher spent the last moments of her life waiting for an earthly pardon that never came and defying a heavenly pardon a minister had offered her. Many believe that very statement trapped her spirit between both worlds. The governor would not pardon her; God wanted to but she refused it; and the devil did not want to hear what message she was bringing. That blasphemous curse left her spirit to return to the last home she had in life, the Old City Jail, and await an earthly pardon before her trial and judgment in the afterlife could begin.

The tale of John and Lavinia Fisher is one of many tales historic Charleston, is famous—or perhaps infamous—for. The legend, in many different forms, has been handed down generation after generation. With each telling, the story has been embellished just a little more. Once again the truth, the paranormal and generations of embellishment became so intertwined that it was hard to separate—until now. The author of this book, Bruce Orr, searched through historical records, archives and eyewitness accounts to separate the fact from the fabrication. Maybe after 190 years the facts need to be reexamined. This book serves that purpose.

It is a well-known fact that justice in Charleston in the 1800s may have been swift but perhaps was not always fair. As Bruce often says, colonial justice was "Fast-Food Justice." They were more interested in quantity served and not quality served.

In reality, in 1820 Lavinia Fisher was sent to the gallows. With her pardon denied and her long white gown fluttering in the breeze, she did indeed scream defiantly in the face of those attempting to lead her to salvation. Her words accompanied by her appearance burned into the minds of everyone in attendance. As the platform dropped, John and Lavinia were not only executed but also launched into legend. The end of their lives is the common ground between the legend and the facts of the case. What leads up to that moment is where the two take distinctly different paths.

What happened then in the name of justice would never be tolerated in this day and age. Things that we take for granted such as freedom and individual rights were subject to the laws of the state. We cannot even fathom the horrors subjected to the Fishers and those like them at the hands of their captors in the Old City Jail. We cannot grasp the cruelties of the Sugar House, where slaves were sent and received punishment—actually more torture than punishment—just because of the color of their skin and the belief they were subservient to their owners. It is a disservice to those who suffered and died in this manner to ignore its harsh realities. History is an opportunity to learn from our mistakes, and colonial Charleston made its fair share of them.

Perhaps the Fishers were one of them.

John LaVerne
Owner, Bulldog Tours

Acknowledgements

I would like to take this opportunity to thank those people who helped me along the way in this endeavor.

John LaVerne, owner of Bulldog Tours in Charleston, South Carolina, for valuable information regarding the legend and for his time in creating the foreword for this book;

David Gobel, artist in Charleston, South Carolina, for his time and the use of his painting, "The Hanging of Lavinia Fisher";

Frank O. Hunt, retired Lowcountry investigative reporter, news anchor and former investigator for the Ninth Circuit Solicitor's Office in Charleston;

Dr. S. Erin McConnell Presnell, Medical University of South Carolina associate professor of pathology, director of medical and forensic autopsy;

Rick Presnell, retired crime scene supervisor/investigator, Charleston County Sheriff's Office;

Sgt. Mike Ringley, former crime scene supervisor/investigator, Charleston County Sheriff's Office;

Michael Murphy, Murphy Whips WA Australia, for his assistance in explaining the weaponry of the period;

Chaplain Ely "Eddie" Driggers, Coastal Carolina Chaplaincy, for his assistance in providing information regarding the Old City Jail and its inhabitants;

Master Deputy William "Bill" Reed III, Charleston County Sheriff's Office, for his assistance in providing information regarding cellars and beer cellars within the Charleston, South Carolina area;

ACKNOWLEDGEMENTS

Suzann Brown and Karen Marr, Bulldog Tours, for their assistance and wealth of knowledge regarding the Old City Jail and John and Lavinia Fisher;

Charleston County Library (68 Calhoun Street, Charleston, SC 29401);

Dorchester County George H. Seago Jr. Library (76 Old Trolley Road, Summerville, SC 29485);

South Carolina Historical Society (100 Meeting Street, Charleston, SC 29401);

South Carolina Department of Archives and History (8301 Parklane Road, Columbia, SC 29223);

Lavinia Fisher (scary coincidence), Italy, for her assistance in researching a possible Italian connection to this legend and for also unnerving me with the strangest coincidence in writing this book;

Alessa Bertoluzzi, Summerville–Dorchester Museum, for rekindling my interest in Lavinia Fisher and her support in this endeavor;

Alkinoos "Ike" Katsilianos, Darkwater Paranormal Investigations, for his insight into the paranormal aspects of the case and discussions into the legitimate facts of the Fishers;

Linda Toporek, Realtor, for her help with property laws and information; and Kayla Orr, photography.

Introduction

Charleston, South Carolina, has such a wonderful and historic past. It has definitely made its mark on the history of this nation. From the very beginning, in 1670 with its original colony, through the first shots of the Civil War at Fort Sumter, to present day, it continues that tradition. Charleston is rich in heart, heritage and history.

Charleston is also rich in legend.

For every Revolutionary War hero, there is an equally despised British villain, and for every Civil War legend, there is a nasty nemesis—usually a Yankee. Within this city, there are a great number of skeletons in the closets—or in this case, in the cellar.

According to legend, John and Lavinia Fisher ran the Six Mile House, an inn on the outskirts of Charleston, South Carolina, in 1819. The couple worked as a criminal team; they are considered the predecessor of murderous couples such as Bonnie and Clyde, whose robbery spree in the 1930s left several dead, nine of them lawmen, or Gerald and Charlene Gallego, who murdered ten victims in the 1970s. Although their death count in legend is much higher, their methods are considered more along the lines of the geriatric couple, Ray and Faye Copeland, who were sentenced for murdering numerous transients who stopped at their farm seeking work. Ray Copeland, age seventy-six, and his wife Faye, age sixty-nine, were convicted of five murders and are believed to have been responsible for at least seven more.

As the legend has it, Lavinia Fisher lured in many guests with her seductive wiles, fed them a fine home-cooked dinner, and then sedated them with warm tea poisoned with oleander. Her husband, John, then robbed them in their sleep, murdered them, butchered them and then disposed of their bodies in the cellar of Six Mile House. It was not until one of their victims escaped, rode into town and alerted the Charleston authorities that their treachery was revealed. Between twenty to thirty victims were alleged to have been found in various states of decomposition in the cellar. Fisher and his wife were charged with those murders and hanged for their crimes.

Later Lavinia, in an effort to provoke sympathy, requested to be hanged in her wedding dress. As she stood on the gallows with her long white dress blowing in the breeze, her defiant last words were, "Cease! I will have none of it. Save your words for others that want them. But if you have a message you want to send to Hell, give it to me; I'll carry it."

As the noose was placed around her neck, she leapt to her death to steal the privilege of her execution from the hangman. So the legend goes.

As a child, I first became acquainted with the legend of John and Lavinia Fisher in a book titled "Charleston Ghosts" by Margaret Rhett Martin. Her story, "The Wayfarer at Six Mile House," quickly became my favorite. It also became a source of nightmares as those creepy skeletons managed to escape John and Lavinia's cellar and find their way under my bed at 3:00 a.m. After a few repeat performances, my father convinced my mother that Ms. Martin's book needed to be confiscated in their efforts to remedy the skeletons' nightly visits. She removed the book and saved me from becoming another of Lavinia's hapless victims—or one of my father's.

Many years passed; I grew up and entered the field of law enforcement. That career would bring me face to face with more than one decomposing corpse in the hot Charleston sun. No longer did the skeletons come to visit me by crawling out from under my bed at 3:00 a.m. I was often called to crawl out of my bed at that time to go visit them. I am now retired, and we both have a standing agreement not to visit each other at all. If they don't haunt me, I won't try to figure out who converted them to skeletons. I will leave that to South Carolina's finest.

Just like it did with me, the tale of the evil Lavinia Fisher and her murderous husband, John, has interested both the residents and visitors of Charleston, South Carolina, for the better part of two centuries now. There are as many versions of the tale as there are tour guides, but one thing is for certain: it is one of the longest lasting and enduring legends of the Lowcountry.

Much has been written about the legend of the pair and their association to an inn known as Six Mile House that existed just outside the city limits of Charleston in 1819. Most of what has been published is strictly legend. The stories are taken from accounts handed down from generation to generation for the past 190 years. With each telling, the story has been embellished just a little more until the actual events of the time were obscured by sensationalism. That is the fantasy of legend. The truth is that little is known of the facts pertaining to the Fishers or the events said to have occurred at Six Mile House.

I have read that Lavinia Fisher was the first female serial killer; the first woman executed in the United States; a witch; a seductress; the creator of a tea to *die* for; and apparently a fashion diva who was hanged in her wedding dress. I have read John Fisher was a coward, died like a dog and had to be dragged to the gallows. In the end, he put all the blame on Lavinia—so legend has it. I have read that as a husband and wife team the two robbed and murdered upward of twenty-plus people as the unsuspecting victims entered and left the city of Charleston conducting business in the wagon trade.

Factually, what is the truth behind the legend? Are there any records still in existence pertaining to the criminal case, and if they do exist, what story do those documents tell?

It is true Lavinia and John Fisher did exist and were associated with Six Mile House. They were arrested and eventually sentenced to death in the courts of Charleston. But what really happened?

It is my intention to separate the fact from fiction and allow the reader to draw one's own conclusion based on those facts—facts of the time in which they occurred. I have taken information from sources that existed at the time, eyewitness accounts, court documents and later sources that used accurate documentation. Some references used will be transcribed in their entirety. Article by article, note by note, bit by bit, a different story unfolded, and the legend of Six Mile House began to unravel. Slowly a different story emerges—a story based in fact.

Most people hear of the legend during haunted tours or ghost walks through the city; therefore, one cannot address the legend without first addressing the paranormal aspects of the story. Lavinia's ghost is supposed to haunt the Old City Jail at 21 Magazine Street and the Unitarian Church Cemetery on Archdale Street. I have been to both and have yet to encounter her. One would think that because I am writing a book about her it would merit a response, but, alas, she has digressed at being interviewed.

In 2006, I met Alessa Bertoluzzi, who reintroduced me to the legend of Lavinia. Alessa is affiliated with the Summerville–Dorchester Museum and has become a good friend and supporter of this book. At that time we were both members of a local paranormal group of which I had the dubious honor of being thrown out of. If you want to do a paranormal investigation, then you need to invite a seasoned, skeptical investigator—me. If you want to do a "ghost hunt," take pictures of dust bunnies and call them orbs, record mouse sneezes and swear they are disembodied spirits speaking to you and automatically rubberstamp everything as "haunted," then please do not invite me. I debunked their investigation, their photographs and their EVPs (electronic voice phenomenon), much to their horror, and was subsequently voted out of the group, much to my delight.

When it comes to the paranormal, I do have an active interest. I also have my own conclusions. Paranormal means something beyond the norm. When all normal avenues of an occurrence have been examined and are found not to be the cause, then a paranormal situation exists. Something other than normal conditions created the event. Paranormal does not equal ghost. Frankly, I have investigated those things, and to me, the jury is still out on them. I am not a ghost hunter. I am an investigator and a researcher. Investigations and research can be applied to all fields, including the paranormal. In fact, with that type of approach, many "hauntings" are debunked. True paranormal investigation is not ghost hunting. Ghost hunters believe that every orb is a spirit, and every place they visit is indeed haunted. Paranormal investigators explore all aspects. They are skeptical, and skepticism makes an excellent investigative tool. Not every orb is a ghost, and the phantom smell you are experiencing could very well be the burrito your partner had two hours earlier.

Along the way, I met Ike Katsilianos of Darkwater Paranormal Investigations. Ike is skeptical, but open-minded. He has a military background and is not too easily convinced that a ghost lurks behind every tombstone in Charleston. He asked me to become involved with his group in researching fact and separating it from fiction. It was something I had always done in criminal investigations, and it was very easy to adapt to the paranormal. Ike and I began to discuss some of the problems with many of the local legends. One of those discussions included the John and Lavinia Fisher legend and the probability that most of the truth of the case died with them. As an investigator, I felt that there had to be a paper trail. I don't care when the events occurred, the fact that a married couple who robbed and murdered their guests and were executed for it means it's going to be documented somewhere. There would be too much public interest for it not to be. There had to be reports; there had to be criminal records. Thus the quest for the Fisher facts began.

Although this is not an examination of the paranormal, I will admit more than one bizarre event has accompanied the research of this book. Many personal experiences occurred at the Old City Jail on my many trips there. Upward of ten thousand people are believed to have died on that spot, so if there is the possibility for a haunting that location is the candidate with the most qualifications.

The most bizarre experience with this book occurred one night while using the Internet in an effort to locate some overseas assistance in my research. The researcher was located and the information in regard to what I was looking for was forwarded. The next morning, the e-mail response was stunning. There is nothing stranger than waking up one morning, opening your e-mail and receiving a message from Lavinia Fisher. I actually spilled my coffee. My young newfound Italian friend (she looks remarkably lovely for someone who died almost two hundred years ago) did assist me in the information I requested; although it is a mere coincidence that the names are the same, one cannot help but concede that it is truly a bizarre one.

Again with that being said, this book is not an investigation into the paranormal. It is not my intention to prove or disprove that the ghost of Lavinia Fisher exists. I will leave that to Ike and others to do. This book has nothing to do with ghosts whatsoever. My intentions here are to reexamine all of the available information of the case that I could find and separate fact from fiction. Truth is what I had hoped to find. This book is a step-by-step documentation of what transpired at Six Mile House, what was occurring during the time of this event and what happened in the aftermath.

What began as a part-time project for a retired criminal investigator turned into a three-year endeavor into the facts of the case. One article would reveal a name that would lead to another record that would lead to another archive, etc., etc. That is what happens in an investigation. One piece of evidence points to the next. One witness account is corroborated by another, and on and on the process goes until the investigator begins to see a picture of the events as they unfolded. Eventually the truth gets sifted and separated from what has been created and fabricated. That is what happened here, and to be frank, I was surprised at the results. As I combed old newspapers, microfiche and archives searching for records, a different story began to emerge. It was a story far different from the one I had read so many years ago as a child or even the ones I debated with my friends as an adult.

In 1819, a crime was alleged to have been committed by the Fishers. An arrest was made; a case was formed; a trial occurred where a verdict was rendered; a sentence was passed; and a punishment was executed. That is what occurred. That chain of events is exactly what should occur in any criminal investigation regardless of the time—1819 is no different than today. That is the path justice should follow regardless. This book will review what transpired in this case from the incident to the punishment based on the facts at hand.

What started as a curious hobby researching two vile murderers eventually turned into an investigation that completely changed my mind in regard to what actually happened. It is my hope that you too will take what is revealed here through actual accounts and separate the fact from the fiction. I hope that this book actually reveals the truth of Six Mile House and the story of John and Lavinia Fisher will no longer be lost in legend.

CHAPTER 1

The Time

1819

In order to understand what occurred with the Fishers, one must first understand the times in which they were living. This chapter will give you a perspective of the events surrounding 1819 and how those events were affecting not only Charleston, but the country as well.

To give you an idea of exactly where 1819 fell within this country's history, let's take a minute and pinpoint it using historical characters and events. In 1819, Davy Crockett was still fighting Indians and was two years away from becoming a member of the Tennessee legislature. He had not yet met his fate at the Alamo. Another historical pioneer, Daniel Boone, was still alive but would die the following year. This was long before westward movement, the Indian Removal Act of 1830 or Custer and Crazy Horse at the Battle of Little Bighorn in 1876. The War of 1812 had ended, and the Civil War, which would start in Charleston, was still decades away.

In 1819, the threat of Indian attacks was a legitimate one. President James Monroe, the fifth president of the United States, had been engaged in issues with the Seminole and the Creek tribes and had ordered Andrew Jackson to war against them. The following year the president would be engaged in treaty negotiations with another Native American faction, the Choctaw. The threat of Indians was a legitimate fear for most of the country. Since the colonization of the country, it always had been. Although the threat was not as prevalent during that year, Charleston had faced its own Indian massacres in its past.

In 1819, Florida was newly acquired, and President Monroe was also busy ironing out disputes with the Spanish colonies with the Treaty of 1819. This year also included a visit by President Monroe to Charleston, a move that may have directly affected the Fishers and what happened to them. In 1819, Missouri sought statehood as a slave state, while Maine was declared a free state. Slavery was still a major source of labor in the United States, although the country was beginning to see its first divisions regarding the issue—a division that would eventually split the nation into North and South.

If the embers of division over slavery were just beginning to glow, kindling was about to be added to it. Congress would authorize President Monroe to send vessels to suppress the African slave trade in 1819 and in the following year Congress would define the slave trade as piracy. The slave trade had always been important to Charleston, and in fact, the city had been one of the largest, if not the largest, slave markets in the country. This fact caused the slave population to rapidly grow in Charleston. The 1790 census listed 15,402 whites to 51,585 blacks. The reality was that the whites of Charleston were the minority in the population; these growing numbers of slaves would continue to rise. This would lead to new laws and tougher restrictions on the slaves known as the "Negro Act." Tighter curfews were enforced, and a slave (all of whom had their owners' surnames as part of their names) caught past curfew without his owner's written permission would find himself making a trip to the "Sugar House." Sometimes a "valuable" slave's master was sent for although most stayed until their masters came searching for them.

The Sugar House was an old sugar warehouse that now served as a prison and a "correctional" facility for errant slaves. What is meant by correctional is that they would be tortured into compliance. A slave taken to the Sugar House may spend the rest of the night being chained to a post and whipped as a reminder not to repeat the infraction. By the time his master located him and paid the fine, the slave was practically useless. Many owners knew this and left the slaves there. If the errant slave was not claimed in sixty days, he could be sold to pay for his room and board.

Ironically, whipping was probably the most preferable treatment inside the confines of the place, for within the walls of the Sugar House was a giant treadmill that was used for grinding corn. The treadmill was powered by slave labor continually pushing the treadmill around the clock. Black overseers with whips made sure the treadmill kept going. Many a tired slave fell, was dragged into and under the contraption and lost a limb or two; several had lost their lives. The contaminated grain would be gathered up at this point and separated, and the process would start again. The contaminated grain containing bits of freshly ground slave were used to feed the imprisoned slaves of the Sugar House and the prisoners of the City Jail.

The site of the Sugar House, in the vicinity of 15 Magazine Street, was also a place of execution for slave crimes. What better place to make an example than on the lawn of the facility that housed those who may become repeat offenders? One such example occurred in 1769 when two slaves, Dolly and Liverpoole, were executed for poisoning a white infant in their care and the attempted poisoning of the child's mother. Liverpoole had been discovered to have supplied the poison, and Dolly had administered it. They both were burned alive on the jailhouse grounds as both punishment for their crimes and as a deterrent for those who dared to think of harming their masters.

Such treatment did not endear the slave owners to the slave population. Animosity ran high. Charleston had already experienced an attempted slave uprising in 1720 and had endured an actual rebellion in 1739 near the Stono River. The Stono Rebellion, as it was called, resulted in the murders of twenty whites. This had been the catalyst that led to the stricter laws of the Negro Act. With the continually increasing numbers of blacks, the citizens of Charleston were again in fear of rebellion during 1819. In fact, in 1822, there would be discovered a conspiracy of a very organized slave uprising and revolt. Denmark Vesey, a local slave, and many of his associates would go to the gallows. Estimates have it that upward of ten thousand blacks had been recruited into Vesey's Rebellion in one fashion or another. In 1819, Denmark Vesey was already fanning the flames of dissention, and the white slave owners, the Negro Act laws and the Sugar House only fueled those flames.

In 1819, the country was experiencing its first economic issues. What would be known as the Panic of 1819 was actually the first major financial crisis this country had ever felt. It was largely caused by the end of economic expansion after the War of 1812 (which ended in 1815). Ironically, much like the events of the twenty-first century, the war had caused economic collapse. Bank failures, foreclosures and unemployment were high; marketing, manufacturing and farm exporting had slumped; and European demand was decreased because Europe had reached a state where agricultural and farming industries had recovered after being destroyed by the Napoleonic War. In the Charleston paper, the *Charleston Courier*, dated June 2, 1819, an article with the headline "Alarming Times" ran as follows:

> *Never within the recollection of our oldest citizens, has the aspect of the times, as it respects property and money, been so alarming. Already has property been sacrificed, in considerable quantities, in this and neighbouring* [sic] *counties, for less than half its value. We have but little money in circulation, and that little is daily diminishing.*

The city was concerned with the diminishing value of their properties, civil judgments and executions in the amount of "many hundred thousand dollars" were hanging over the heads of many. They further lamented that warrants, writs and judgments would soon far outnumber the amount of currency in circulation. The city looked to the state, the state looked to the country and no one seemed to have an answer to the economic crisis. Many feared that Charleston would soon be reduced to a city of beggars, vagrants, thieves and cutthroats.

It appeared that the concerns of the citizens of Charleston had a legitimate basis. Exports from Charleston were dwindling, but those that did leave the ports were not guaranteed safe passage. Unfortunately piracy was still quite prevalent in the waters in and about the Charleston harbor. Many ships became "patriots" of other countries and committed piracy under the flags of those countries. Pirates no longer flew their own personal flags. Flags such as the Jolly Roger with its skull and crossbones were now highly recognizable and even to this day that particular flag has become the trademark symbol of piracy. This new age of piracy realized their own personal flags and banners attracted too much undesired attention, so they learned to be more discreet and often downright covert. In fact, one such enterprising pirate, Captain George Clark, had commanded the *Louisa* under the flag of Buenos Aires. In 1819, he and members of his crew were housed in the city's jail and were awaiting trial for piracy.

The *Louisa* had been a privateer vessel under the command of Captain Joseph Almeina in the War of 1812. Its armament had been ten guns, and the ship had been manned with forty men. It now boasted sixteen guns and a total of eighty-six men. Under Captain Almeina's command, it had captured a Spanish vessel, and he placed the ship under the command of his lieutenant, Mr. Smith, as he himself left with a boarding party. The gunner, George Clark (also called Craig), took advantage of this moment and took over the ship in a mutiny. The officers of the vessel who remained in support of the previous captain were confined. They were eventually released to a French freighter. Now under Clark's command, the *Louisa* wreaked havoc on the seas. They attacked first a British ship and then an American ship loaded with freight from France. They then sailed to the Isle of May, an island off the coast of Scotland. Once there, Clark plundered two American vessels harbored there—the *Charles* from New York and the *Boston* from Alexandria, Virginia. The raid went so well that they then continued on to plunder the entire town.

They were doing so well that they then set sail toward America and, along the way, plundered a Russian ship, a French vessel and another two

American vessels, one bound for Rio de Janeiro and the other from Boston bound for Havana. Up until now, Clark had done surprisingly well and had been amazingly lucky in his endeavors as a pirate. Now, to his misfortune, his luck was about to change. By now the *Louisa* had suffered damage in the attacks and was also being searched for. Clark noted a passing ship and pretended to be disabled and distressed. The ship cautiously moved in to investigate. Clark met with the American schooner from North Carolina and sent all his crew on board except for about twenty-five. Rest assured he used the pretext that his ship had been attacked by pirates. The unsuspecting North Carolina vessel accepted the crew in this heroic "rescue," not realizing that they were actually pirates themselves and not victims. Clark's ruse worked well for his crew.

Captain Clark and this current handful of men stayed behind and scuttled the ship off the coast of Charleston. They turned its own guns upon the ship, set it on fire and left it in flames. The men and Clark then took lifeboats from the vessel and rowed ashore. They then proceeded to Charleston. Their intent was to plunder Charleston much as they had the Isle of May. Unfortunately Captain Clark's reign of piracy would come to an end in Charleston in 1819, and his life would come to an end in March 1820 at the end of a rope.

Piracy was not the only threat that Charleston faced from the sea. In June 1819, a yellow fever epidemic forced Governor John Geddes to issue a quarantine proclamation against vessels arriving at Charleston. The vessels were to drop anchor at Fort Johnson and be inspected prior to sailing into Charleston. The commanding officer of Fort Johnson was ordered to enforce this quarantine, with arms and firepower if necessary, against any vessel violating the proclamation. This created further problems for shipping, and the newly appointed governor had his hands full.

Fortunately there was the wagon trade.

Wagons loaded with materials traveled far and wide to reach the Carolina coast. It was not unusual for hides, cotton or tobacco to travel three or four hundred miles to market in efforts to reach the wagon yards of Charleston. While the economy may have been bad and exports dwindling, farmers, trappers and traders still flocked to Charleston to sell their products.

The trips were long and tiresome. Horses wearied and so did their owners. Teams of six to eight horses were needed to pull the loads to market. They needed places along the route to stop and rest and receive water. These places took form in the stage taverns or inns known as "Houses" that dotted the roadways on the outskirts of towns and cities. These inns were usually

In 1819, ships such as these were becoming less of a common site as commerce slowed, and piracy still continued. *Courtesy of author.*

designated by the distance from the appointed destination. The Four Mile House was, of course, approximately four miles from Charleston. Five Mile House, Six Mile House, Ten Mile House were likewise and so on. Eventually the inns and taverns took on other names in the following years, but the mile marker designations seemed to endure. Most still endure to this day.

The stagecoach taverns or houses were not what we imagine an inn or tavern to be today. The countryside inns or taverns were more social centers for the countryside. The latest news and gossip was spread by passengers to the taverns and later diffused to the people of the city. The inner-city inns and taverns served food and drink and provided lodging. These were more of what one considers an inn to be today.

Of course being a proprietor of one, or several, of these inns could be advantageous. Traders, avoiding the higher costs of the city, may take advantage of your inns. If you were an honest proprietor, you could make a fair wage taking care of your customers. Add the care of the horses and the price goes up.

A map of the Charleston district by Robert Mills, dated 1825, actually has several of the taverns locations denoted. Six Mile House, rebuilt after being destroyed by fire six years earlier, was a little beyond the intersection of Goose Creek Road, now Highway 52 or Rivers Avenue, and Dorchester Road. The Four Mile House was, of course, a little closer to the city.

The Four Mile House is often, erroneously, said to be the location of the Fishers' crimes. In the *South Carolina Historical and Genealogical Magazine* (volume 19, January 1918–January 1919), it appears that Judge Henry Augustus Middleton Smith identified the Four Mile House as being upon a tract known as Discher Farm. That is true but then he states, inaccurately, that it was the scene of the incidents with the Fishers. His confusion may be due to the fact that the Four Mile House was originally called the Six Mile House in the 1700s, not the 1800s when the incidents took place in the location ran by the Fishers. The first mention of the place Smith is referring to being called the Four Mile House Tract is in a 1786 deed of sale from James Donovan to John Bowen.

According to research, the Four Mile House was demolished in October 1969 after several efforts were made in a four-year effort by the preservation society to maintain it as a landmark. The house and its four-acre plot were purchased by the Milton F. Truluck Trust and was the remaining portion of the seventy-acre plot on which the inn was built. Edward Evans, a member of the demolition firm, was interviewed and stated that he saw no hidden compartments, trapdoors or cellars on or around the house during the demolition.

Leaving Charleston along what was once Goose Creek Road, one can locate Discher Road and Four Mile Road. They are apparently the only reminders left of the Four Mile House and its seventy-acre tract.

A little over a mile from that location is Five Mile Viaduct. A little over two miles from there behind Whipper Barony subdivision is an area known as Seven Mile and lastly, at the Intersection of Highway 52 (Rivers Avenue) and Remount Road is a business park known as Ten Mile Station. Although the taverns have been long gone, it is obvious that the mileage designations created back then are still used to this day.

In overlaying and comparing plat 6881 and a current map, one gets a general idea of where Six Mile House was. The Six Mile House would have been in an area now occupied by the Charleston Naval Health Clinic, previously known as the Charleston Naval Hospital. This nestles it directly between and across from the Charleston County Sheriff's Office and the North Charleston Police Department Substation. It is quite ironic, and

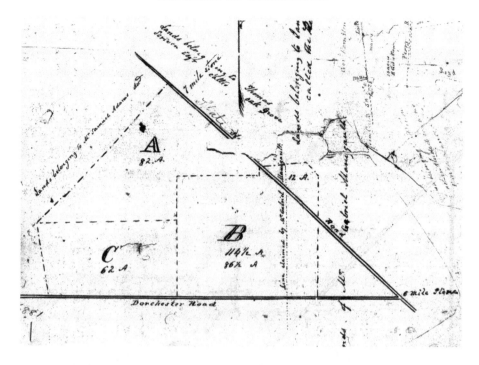

Above: Plat 6881 shows the location of Six Mile House near the intersection of Dorchester Road and Goose Creek Road, which is now Rivers Avenue. *Courtesy South Carolina Department of Archives and History.*

Left: Four Mile Lane in the vicinity of where Four Mile House once stood. *Courtesy of author.*

somewhat humorous, that this legend of one of the most vicious female serial killers in the state of South Carolina originated on the very doorstep of not one but two of this state's largest law enforcement agencies. What is even more ironic is that one of those agencies evolved from the elected

Discher Street where Discher Farm once stood, a tract containing Four Mile House. *Courtesy of author.*

Five Mile Viaduct where Five Mile House once stood. *Courtesy of author.*

The Charleston Naval Clinic, formerly the Charleston Naval Hospital, now sits where Six Mile House once stood. *Courtesy of author.*

position of the person who arrested the Fishers. The Office of Sheriff of Charleston back then is now known as the Charleston County Sheriff's Office today. This agency now employs hundreds of deputies and is divided into numerous specialized divisions.

With the wagon and stage trade prevalent, the traders themselves became targets for highway robbery. If a full wagon was heading into town, one could easily hijack the wagon and take the goods for themselves. If one were leaving town with an empty wagon, then one could assume that the goods had been sold and the trader was carrying cash.

In the early months of 1819, highwaymen were busy. A citizen, James Addison, had been robbed of a little over $10.00 at dusk by a white man mounted on a white horse. John Brown had also been robbed and deprived of $140.00. Others had been lured into the inns where they were cheated in crooked gambling games. Added to those complaints was that of Stephen LaCoste, who had gone to his pasture to check on his cow and found the creature missing. Mr. LaCoste was quite certain the cow had not wandered off and had met with a much more diabolical fate.

Those involved in the wagon trade, along with anyone else traveling to and from Charleston, felt it necessary to carry their rifles for protection. This frustrated the citizenry of Charleston, and they had had more than enough. They feared that the news of such robberies would deter trade and create even more problems to the already failing Charleston commerce. Younger and smaller towns such as Cheraw, Camden, Columbia and Hamburg were already in a position to intercept the wagon trade, and the threat of robbery was sure to divert these merchants to these smaller towns and their smaller wagon yards.

On February 16, 1819, a mob set out from Charleston to take the matters into their own hands. Well armed, determined and riding under their own authority, they set out for the Five Mile House. They set forth under "Lynch's Law" and no other authority at all.

The term Lynch's Law was used as early as 1782. A prominent Virginian named Charles Lynch created his own laws and terms in suppressing a suspected loyalist uprising in 1780 during the Revolutionary War. The suspects were given a trial at an informal court. The sentences handed down included whipping, property seizure, coerced pledges of allegiance and forced enrollment into the military. Charles Lynch's extralegal actions were retroactively legitimized by the Virginia General Assembly in 1782.

A second explanation of Lynch's Law comes from another source. In 1811, Captain William Lynch claimed that the phrase "Lynch's Law" actually came from a 1780 compact signed by him and his neighbors in Pittsylvania County, Virginia. The compact allowed them to uphold their own brand of law outside of legal authority. Regardless of the origins of Lynch's Law, it was nothing more than mob justice without legal authority. The state of South Carolina eventually created laws against such acts.

Lynching is now a felony. Lynching in the first degree, section 16-3-210 of the South Carolina Code of Laws, deals with the death of a person at the hands of a mob. Any person found guilty of lynching in the first degree shall suffer death unless the jury shall recommend the defendant to the mercy of the court, in which the defendant shall be confined at hard labor in the state penitentiary for a term not exceeding forty years or less than five years at the discretion of the presiding judge.

Lynching in the second degree, section 16-3-220 of the South Carolina Code of Laws, is an act of violence by a mob in which death does not occur. It is a felony and any person found guilty of the crime shall be confined at hard labor in the state penitentiary for a term not exceeding twenty years or less than three years at the discretion of the presiding judge. While lynching in the first degree is rarely used when a charge of murder will suffice, second-degree lynching is still utilized in cases of gang violence within the state. It is considered by investigators to be the state's gang statute. That is exactly what a gang is: it is a mob gathered together in unison to commit violent and criminal acts. Then again, in present-day South Carolina, lynch mobs, or gangs, are illegal. The year of 1819 was quite different. Remember that colonial justice does not equal criminal justice, but we will cover that in a later chapter.

Apparently a gang of these robbers had set up shop in the area of Ashley Ferry just outside of Charleston. The robbers could not be identified by any of the victims, so the lynch mob set out to find and disband the group and force them away from the inns in the area. They allegedly had permission from the owners of several small houses in the area to proceed as they saw fit. The fact that the Charleston newspaper, the *Courier*, reports that this group set forth to find and drive away a group they could not even identify is quite interesting.

The mob arrived at a house commonly called the Five Mile House and found a small group gathered there. The group was ordered to vacate the premises and was given fifteen minutes to comply. When they protested, resisted and failed to comply in leaving the building, the lynch mob responded by setting the building on fire. In a very short time it burned to the ground along with some adjacent outbuildings. The Five Mile House was completely destroyed.

The lynch mob then reorganized and proceeded farther up the road to Six Mile House to repeat the process. The same order was given to vacate, and this time the occupants thought it best to comply quickly. Rest assured that the smoke and ash in the February air blowing from the remains of Five Mile House was incentive enough. So were the warnings of its former occupants. After the occupants had departed and the Six Mile House was vacant, the lynch mob placed a young man inside to watch over the property. That man's name was David Ross.

Armed under the pretext of Lynch's Law, the mob had ridden out from Charleston first to the Five Mile House and, after administering their own brand of justice, they then proceeded to the Six Mile House to do the same. They had no legal authority and were not represented by such in any way. Documentation also shows that not one of the robbery victims could identify any of their assailants. Regardless of these facts, the lynch mob returned to Charleston with the feeling they had successfully and completely driven out and disbanded the occupants of both inns. An account of their actions was reported in the *Charleston Courier* on Saturday, February 20, 1819.

CHAPTER 2

The Victims

TWO CORPSES AND A COW

Sometime after the lynch mob returned to Charleston, the occupants that had been driven out of the Six Mile House returned to the inn. An altercation occurred with David Ross as he stood guard over the Six Mile House. He was attacked but managed to escape into the woods and make his way back to town. His sworn affidavit, given to the authorities on February 20, 1819, described what transpired according to Ross.

> *David Ross being duly sworn deposeth that on yesterday about the hour of nine, William Hayward came to Six Mile House of which he was in possession, accompanied by another person, whose name is unknown by him, that the said Hayward cursed him, collared him violently, and pushed him out of doors. The deponent then again reentered the house, and asked to take away the few articles that belonged to him; Hayward put his hand into his bosom, and said you damned infernal rascal, if you lay your hand on anything, I will blow your brains out.—By this time Fisher and his wife Lavinia Fisher came up, with two other men, whose names are unknown to him—that Lavinia Fisher laid violent hands upon him, choaked [sic] and boxed his head through a pain [sic] of window glass—whilst I was endeavoring to get away from them, Hayward and Fisher beat him unmercifully, with loaded whips aided and assisted by the other two men, whose names are unknown to him, there was also another woman, who aided and assisted, whilst they were beating him, the deponent leapt out of the piazza, and crossed the road through the woods then he got to the Four Mile House, but just as he had entered the woods,*

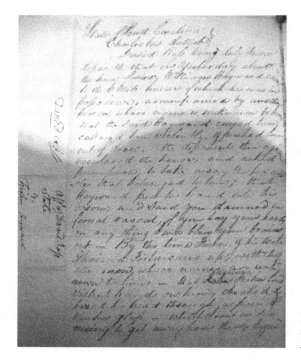

First page of David Ross's statement. *Courtesy South Carolina Department of Archives and History.*

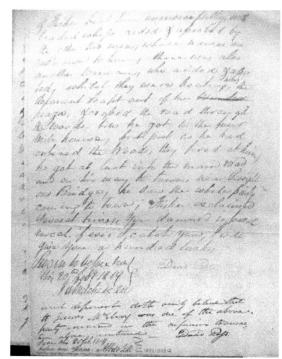

Second page of David Ross's statement. *Courtesy South Carolina Department of Archives and History.*

they fired at him, he got at least into the main road and on his way to town, near Freightous Bridge, he saw the whole party coming to town, Fisher exclaimed several times, you damned infernal rascal if ever I catch you, I will give you a hundred lashes.

As an amendment, the following appears to have been added after the judge's signature: "and deponent doth believe that James McElroy was one of the above party concerned in the nefarious transactions above mentioned."

As David Ross was making his way back to town after the alleged attack, a trader named John Peoples was making his way out of town. Two hours after Ross was attacked, Peoples stopped at the Six Mile House to water his horses. As he and a young boy that was with him watered the horses, he was allegedly attacked and robbed. The following is the affidavit that Peoples provided to the authorities upon his return to Charleston.

John Peeples being duly sworn deposeth that on yesterday forenoon, the 19th into about eleven o'clock as he was returning home from town to his residence in the country he stopped near the forks of the road about 6 miles from town to water his horse that whilst his horses were watering a man came out of the 6 Mile House and told a boy who was with him that he must give him his bucket as he wanted to water his horse, the boy refused to give him the bucket saying he wanted it himself, he swore he would have it and immediately nine or ten persons, among them a tall, stout woman, came out of the same house to the place where he was armed with clubs, guns, and pistols, and immediately made a violent assault on him, some of them beating him with sticks and with their guns, and several times they flashed their pistols at him, that the woman appeared to be the most active in beating him, cutting him over the head and eyes with a stick—that after a while they left him, and reentered the same house, and the deponent proceeded about two hundred yards on the road when two of the same men came up to him on horseback, and stopped his waggon [sic]—and said to him that they would kill him, both of them presenting pistols to him and snapped them at him and demanded of him his money, they then searched his pocket, and took out his pocketbook, which contained his money amounting to between thirty five and forty dollars and then rode back towards the house from whence they came, the Six Mile House—the deponent then came back to Charleston—the deponent doth not know the names of those persons who hath so cruelly beat him and robbed him but that he hath just cause to believe that among them was William Hayward, John Fisher and his wife Lavinia Fisher, Joseph Roberts and John Andrews.

First page of John Peoples's statement. *Courtesy South Carolina Department of Archives and History.*

to be the most active in beating
him, striking him over the head
& eyes with a stick — that after
a while they left him, & reentered the
same house, and the deponent pro
ceeded on the road with his Waggon,
that he had proceeded about two hundred
yards on the road, when two of the
same men came up to him, on horse
back, & stopped his Waggon — and
said to him, that they would kill him,
both of them presenting pistols to him
and snapped them at him, & deman
ded of him, his money, they then search
ed his pockets, and took out his pocket
book, which contained his money,
amounting to between thirty five
and forty dollars, & then rode back
towards the house from whence they
came, the Six mile house — the depo
nent then came back to Charleston
the deponent doth not Know the Names
of those persons, who had so cruelly
beat him & robbed him but that he has
just cause to believe, that among

Second page of John Peoples's statement. *Courtesy South Carolina Department of Archives and History.*

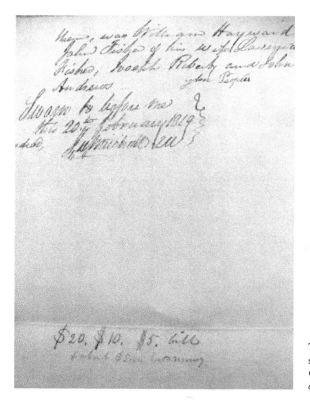

Third page of John Peoples's statement. *Courtesy South Carolina Department of Archives and History.*

Some interesting things to note about Peoples's affidavit are that it is written in several different forms of handwriting and his name is spelled both as "Peeples" and "Peoples." It is signed "John Peoples." Included on the affidavit is a list:

6 Mile Housemen
John Fisher
Lavinia Fisher
Wm. Hayward
Joseph Roberts
Wm. Andrews
Seth Young
James McElroy
John Smith
F. Davis
James Sterrett

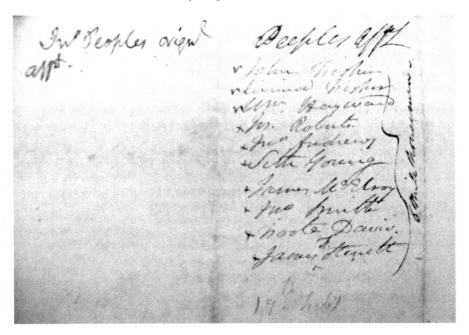

Side note on Peoples's statement listing Six Mile Housemen. *Courtesy South Carolina Department of Archives and History.*

Davis's first name is unreadable, and his arrest is undocumented. It appears that these names were added to the affidavit much as James McElroy's name had been added to Ross's affidavit. Both affidavits were sworn out at the same time by the same judge. Since the signature is different in spelling than the actual affidavit and the handwriting is different, it is obvious this statement was written for John Peoples. It is also in the same handwriting as David Ross's affidavit.

With two victims, the sheriff was now moved into action where he had failed to take action before. With a fairly large "Party of gentlemen," as the *Charleston Courier* would later report, the sheriff, Colonel Nathaniel Greene Cleary, set out to the Six Mile House. Upon surrounding the house, the occupants surrendered without a fight and were taken into custody, even though they had been armed with ten to twelve muskets and a keg of powder. Many accounts state John Fisher opted to surrender rather than risk injury or death to his wife, Lavinia. That is one account. Another version is apparently the large group surrounding the house put a quick end to any thoughts of resistance. Regardless of the reasoning for lack of resistance,

John and Lavinia Fisher, James McElroy, Seth Young and Jane Howard were taken into custody, loaded into the paddy wagon and taken to the City Jail on Magazine Street. While searching the property, the sheriff's group located the hide of a cow that had been killed recently. The hide had been hidden inside an outhouse. It was indeed identified as a cow belonging to Stephen LaCoste, one of Charleston's citizens. He had been correct in his belief that it had met with a very unpleasant fate.

The sheriff's group then set fire to the Six Mile House, and it was burned to the ground, including all outbuildings. No one was allowed to remove anything. Absolutely everything was burned, just as the Five Mile House had been burned the night before.

Located behind the Old City Jail on Magazine Street is a very large iron paddy wagon that had been used in Charleston since the 1700s. This wagon would have been used to bring the prisoners to the jail. The enormous weight of the paddy wagon required at least eight large draft horses to pull it. The open cage allowed spectators to throw rotted fruit and garbage at the accused as they were taken to jail. The six-mile ride back to Charleston in

Paddy wagon used to transport prisoners in Charleston. The open cage allowed objects to be thrown at prisoners by spectators. *Courtesy of author.*

The Fishers' introduction to colonial justice began at the rear entry to the paddy wagon.
Courtesy of author.

the cold February air had to be bad. Add in the fact that it was inside a cast-iron cage on dirt and cobblestone roads—it had to make the trip grueling. It apparently was the beginning of a very harsh existence for the Fishers inside the city jail.

This story is quite a different one from the legend. The statements of both victims have been furnished in their entirety just as they were written. There are no accounts of trapdoors, poisoned tea or a cellar full of skeletons. In fact, quite a lot of research went into trying to document the numerous bodies alleged to have been uncovered in the cellar. Legend has it that the cellar was uncovered in June 1819 and that numerous skeletal remains were found. A member of the gang, William Heyward, would later be captured and hanged in August 1820. His charges did not reflect the fact that numerous bodies had been located. Surely with a year and two months' time since this alleged gruesome discovery, the murders would have reached the media and been reflected in the charges against Mr. Heyward. That never happened, and the reason that it never happened is because the story of a cellar full of corpses, just like the oleander poisoned tea, is fabrication and fiction.

A search of the death records of 1819 and 1820 found no such evidence of a mass grave of skeletal remains. No records at all were found even remotely similar to this claim. What was found was an article in the *Charleston Courier* dated February 26, 1819, less than a week after the arrests. It is the only account of bodies contributed or associated with the Six Mile House.

The coroner for the Charleston district was Jervis H. Stevens. He had received information that a fresh grave was found in the woods near the Six Mile House. It was believed that the gang of robbers had buried a man there approximately ten days prior to his receipt of the information. The man had been reported to have been shot to death.

Coroner Stevens went to the location, and during his search, he did indeed locate a fresh grave. Much to his surprise, the excavation of the gravesite revealed not one, but two bodies. The first appeared to have long hair and to be a white male buried in a box made of rough slabs. The other body, which had been located buried beside the first, appeared to be the remains of a young Negro female. The remains of the woman were alleged to have been placed in the grave two years prior. Nothing remained of her but her skeleton. She is the only skeleton associated with Six Mile House. She was not discovered in a cellar. She was simply buried on the property in an unmarked grave, not at all uncommon for slaves in 1819. Today we may find this appalling, but in 1819, this was a daily occurrence.

No one was ever charged with either of these deaths. In fact, the person shot was never attributed to being a victim of any crime at all. Could perhaps he had been a member of the gang who was mortally wounded in a self-defense act by a potential robbery victim? More than likely he was killed in the assault on the Five Mile House or the initial assault on the Six Mile House by the lynch mob. He may have been the missing "F. Davis" or William Andrews listed on Peoples's affidavit.

The *Charleston Courier* article states that the person was said to have been shot about ten days prior. This was February 26. The raids on the Five Mile House and the Six Mile House had occurred on February 18, eight days earlier, putting it in the same time frame. It is highly possible this man was killed in the assault upon the Five Mile House since there was resistance and it was burned to the ground that night in order to drive those occupants out.

The report of the bodies in the *Charleston Courier* is directly below a report of the arrest of John Smith and Joseph Roberts in regard to the gang. It is most likely that the information of the corpses came from them. Since

The body count is greatly exaggerated in the legend. In fact, no murders were ever attributed to the Fishers. *Courtesy of author.*

The oleander tea, the dismembered bodies and even the wedding dress have no basis in fact. *Courtesy of Kayla Orr.*

neither Smith nor Roberts was charged with murder, one can assume that the man in the grave may have been in allegiance with the gang and not their victim.

As the legend has it, the numerous skeletal remains and decomposing corpses had been located in a cellar under the house. Now as far as cellars in Charleston, Charleston is below sea level and has constant drainage and flooding issues. It did then and does continue to have them to this day. That being said, it does not mean that there were none, but the likelihood of a colonial cellar in the area where the Six Mile House stood even on the outskirts of the city is extremely unlikely.

During this time, beer cellars were popular in European countries and used to store kegs and casks of beer and keep them cool. There was, of course, no refrigeration. A below-ground cellar such as a root cellar or a beer cellar most probably would not have existed in the Charleston area.

Most beer cellars in the Charleston area were storage areas above ground and directly under the first floor of the home. The homes that had them were elevated to allow such areas. Had there been a multitude of decaying corpses above ground or even shallowly buried under the home, the smell would have been unbearable. The presence of one rotting corpse in the Charleston summer is not pleasant. A multitude of decaying corpses would be horrendous. Someone would have surely noticed. That is exactly what led to the apprehension of serial killer John Wayne Gacy and the location of the thirty-three decaying corpses he had stuffed in his crawl space and the additional three buried in shallow graves in his yard. The smell just has a way of giving those things away. If Lavinia and John Fisher had murdered that many people, there would have been reports made, and the papers would have reported such disappearances. Again, none were found.

The tale of multiple corpses can be attributed to Peter Neilson. Peter Neilson, a Scot, claimed to have been in Charleston in 1820 when the Fisher ordeal reached its climax. He wrote a book, published in 1830, in which he stated that the Six Mile House gang "had for years carried on a complete trade of murdering and robbing altogether unheard of, except perhaps in Italy in former times." He goes on, further stating, "On digging around this den of iniquity, a great number of skeletons were found, no doubt the remains of unfortunate travelers."

Mr. Neilson would have been familiar with beer cellars in his own homeland. He possibly attributed this "writer's embellishment" to the Six Mile House tavern. His book was ten years after the fact and one begins to question why he would wait so long to report such a horrific find unless he was waiting on the facts to fade and the fantastic to be embraced. Perhaps the real answer lies in what would become known as the "Penny Dreadful."

In the nineteenth century, publications known as Penny Dreadfuls circulated Europe. They were cheap, thus the name. They were also sensational fictional works or overexaggerations of actual events. Our Scottish friend Peter Neilson appears to have been author of such. That would have made it 1830 if he waited ten years after the events. This was actually the height of popularity for these cheap stories. He can be attributed as the direct source of the excessive body count. His Penny Dreadful account of the Fishers boosted their villainy as much as the dime novels in the later 1800s did for outlaws such as Billy the Kid.

With the legend raising the number of victims to incredible levels, Lavinia Fisher is often referred to as America's first female serial killer. From the facts gathered, she does not fit the criteria. The Behavioral Science Unit of the FBI was created by Agent Roy Hazelwood and a handful of others. He was one of the original serial profilers and instrumental in creating the definition of what a serial killer is. It is the FBI who defines the criteria for a person to be identified as a serial killer, and that definition is a person who murders three or more people over a period of more than thirty days with a cooling-off period between each murder. Neither of the two corpses was ever proven to be a victim of anything the Fishers are accused of. The two bodies were never criminally connected with Lavinia Fisher or John Fisher at all. Even if they had been, that is still only two corpses, one less than the definition requires, unless you count the LaCoste cow found in the outhouse.

CHAPTER 3

The Gang

THE FORGOTTEN MEMBERS

A stay in the City Jail, no matter how brief, was not a pleasant one. The City Jail, or as it was referred to back then, "The Gaol," was built in 1802 to replace the Provost Dungeon. It was built over a potter's field cemetery of slaves, vagrants and derelicts. A jail that was built to hold approximately 130 people often held 300 or more. The ancient building has often been described more as a place of torture rather than a jail or correctional facility. One estimate places the deaths at this location in the area of 10,000 or more. Whippings, beatings, physical assaults and sexual assaults were commonplace, and that was with the jailers (or gaolers as they were called) and prisoners alike. The bars on the windows did little to keep out the bone-chilling cold of Charleston's winters or the stifling heat and humidity of the city's summers. It also did little to keep out the insects and rodents that infested the city.

In early times, the most dangerous of the prisoners were secured by being chained to a large ring in the center of the floor. These would be your violent offenders and your escape risks. This also would be the method for securing the severely mentally ill since the jail also served as an insane asylum. In later years, prisoners were kept seven or eight to a cage with a multitude of cages being kept on each floor. There was no separation of the sexes unless the guards removed the females for their own personal entertainment.

There was no running water within the building, so therefore sanitary conditions were deplorable. Within the jail, wood chips were scattered on the floor. That was the prisoner's bedding and quite often their toilet. Occasionally the chips would be changed, but not often. If you had suffered

Left: Old City Jail on Magazine Street where the Six Mile gang was held. *Courtesy of author.*

Below: The cage used to house seven to eight inmates *Courtesy of author.*

at the hands of your tormentors, you were returned to your cell and your open wounds were exposed to the filth of your living conditions. Infection and disease were rampant. What manners of death that were not created by infection, brought in from the harbor, blown in through the windows, carried in by the rats or dealt by the captors was often carried out by the prisoners upon themselves. Suicide was often a preferable fate.

Through the years, the jail underwent many redesigns. In 1822, the architect Robert Mills designed a four-story wing with one-man cells. This was done after public outcry over several escapes of violent prisoners. This wing was taken down in 1855 for the construction of an octagonal wing. That wing was originally four stories with a two-story octagonal tower. The tower and the fourth story were removed in 1886 after being severely damaged in the devastating earthquake that hit Charleston. The jail actually remained in service until 1939.

Punishment for criminal offenses was no picnic either. Colonial punishment was still enforced. Public whippings, or lashings, were inflicted. Whips that were commonly used during that time were referred to as loaded whips. This term is mentioned in David Ross's statement as a weapon having been used

Jailers' quarters. *Courtesy of author.*

The octagonal section was added in 1855, years after the execution of the Fishers *Courtesy of author.*

A section of the jail currently undergoing reconstruction. *Courtesy of author.*

against him. A loaded whip is one that has small lead shot sewn into it to add weight as it is swung. This technique gives you the flexibility of a whip and the force of being hit with a steel rod, accompanied by the lacerating effects of the braided leather. Many prisoners received this treatment, were dragged back to their cells through the urine- and feces-soaked wood shavings and left to die. Once they did die, there was no real hurry to remove them. It was not unusual for a corpse to reach an advanced state of decomposition before being removed. It served as a visual reminder for the prisoners to control themselves. The bodies would eventually be removed and taken to the lower section of the jail to be housed in the morgue.

Branding was also a common punishment. It also was used as an identifier in marking a person as an offender. Much as the character Hester Pryne was forced to wear the letter "A" for being convicted of adultery in Nathaniel Hawthorne's book, *The Scarlett Letter*, many persons were branded with the first letter of their offense. Michael Toohey, a participant in another crime discussed later in this book, was branded with the letter "M" in the palm of his hand. He was convicted of manslaughter. Another person considered to be a member of the Six Mile House gang had been branded for larceny.

Croppings were also used in the same manner. Part of a person's ear or nose may be cut off or cropped as punishment for a crime they committed. One of the gang members, later to be arrested, showed the harsh evidence of this punishment.

The jail was nothing more than a new aboveground dungeon for the city of Charleston and an improved torture chamber. It may not have been as damp or flooded as bad as the old dungeon, but it had much the same amenities.

During those times the seriousness of the crime was in the eyes of the colonial justice system. The punishment was at the discretion of the judge. A conviction of manslaughter resulting in the death of another may get you branded like Michael Toohey, while an offense of Negro stealing would get you hanged. If the offense was considered serious enough, forfeiting your life was not uncommon back then. The charges facing those associated with the Five Mile House and the Six Mile House were considered egregious enough. Colonial justice does not equal criminal justice. Although the country was moving away from the colonial justice system, Charleston was slow to follow.

As of Monday morning, February 22, 1819, the sheriff, Colonel Nathanial Greene Cleary, had John and Lavinia Fisher, James McElroy, Seth Young, Jane Howard and William Heyward (aka William Hayward or William Howard) in custody, bringing the total to six. The arrests would continue, and the number of the gang members would continue to grow. By that afternoon, James Sterrett would be joining them.

To Sheriff Cleary, James Sterrett was a familiar offender in the city of Charleston. About twelve months prior to this arrest, he had received a branding for a larceny charge. This time he was picked up on a warrant issued by J.H. Mitchell in regard to being a member of the gang and being involved in the assault on David Ross. By the end of the week, the arrests of John Smith and Joseph Roberts would bring the Six Mile House gang's total to nine. They were brought before Mitchell, charged with being accomplices in the gang and committed to jail. The Six Mile gang's trial was set for May in the court of sessions.

William Andrews and F. Davis were never arrested. Remember that these were two of the names that were added to John Peoples's affidavit. Jane Howard was never listed in the court records as one of the suspects, but she was arrested upon Colonel Cleary's arrival at Six Mile House just the same. That makes Lavinia Fisher one of two women associated with the gang and not the sole female as the legend dictates.

One by one the prisoners were brought down to be identified by John Peoples. Remember that according to Peoples's affidavit, it states that, "the deponent doth not know the names of those persons who hath so cruelly beat him and robbed him." Therefore a lineup of sorts had to be performed. According to Colonel Cleary, there were approximately twenty to thirty witnesses to that identification process to ensure that it was not tainted and Peoples was not swayed in any way.

On March 26, 1819, Philip Walker was a victim of a burglary at his home. Walker was a resident of Goose Creek, a city a little over fifteen miles outside of Charleston. The determined thief had gained entry by prying up part of the flooring of the residence. Once inside he located and carried away a small trunk containing $150.00, three silver watches, clothing, a hat and coat. He then stole a horse belonging to Mr. Walker and fled. Mr. Walker later found his horse in the area of Goose Creek Bridge, but did not locate the thief. Mr. Walker was extremely upset and offered a reward for the recovery of his property.

The offender, René Jacobs, was subsequently captured. Jacobs was located that same night by one of Charleston's police officers. As the *Charleston Courier* reported, it was no use for Jacobs to deny the accusations because he was found wearing Walker's clothing that he had stolen from the residence. The paper further contributes him to the gang of "Land Privateersmen" broken up near the Five Mile House. Jacobs is described as a sea-faring man, and the gang's actions are attributed to them having been schooled in the art of "Patriot Privateering." In other words, they were being called pirates. This arrest brought the total to ten in custody and two at large. In total, twelve persons were associated with the gang.

The Six Mile gang was not the only criminal elements that Charleston faced at that particular time. As stated earlier, the pirate captain George Clark and members of his crew were housed in the City Jail. Perhaps the example of his capture and incarceration had forced other Patriot Privateers to take up the art of Land Privateering, as the *Charleston Courier* article stated. Apparently land in the Charleston area was much better suited for robbery than the harbor—until now.

Also housed in the jail was Martin Toohey. Martin Toohey and his gang had murdered James W. Gadsden. Gadsden had been a member of a prominent South Carolina family, but it did not save him from Toohey's knife. Michael Toohey, Martin's brother, had been involved in the crime but received a lesser sentence for manslaughter and received a branding as punishment.

Many of the Six Mile offenders had a criminal history. At twenty-eight years of age, John Fisher had already once been sentenced to receive thirty lashes for theft, but he had been pardoned by the governor on condition he leave not only the city of Charleston but also the entire state of South Carolina.

James Sterrett had been convicted of larceny in Charleston the previous year. He had received a branding as a result.

Joseph Roberts was missing part of his ear. Cropping was still considered as a punishment and apparently he had received this treatment. He had already been held in the jail in 1817 but had escaped the Charleston jail by pretending to belong to a party of visitors. He had also escaped from jail in Savannah, Georgia.

William Heyward was also familiar with the courts of Charleston. He was quite the busy fellow. In 1815, he and a female accomplice were indicted for assault and robbery. He was accused of assaulting Jane Francis, stripping the clothes from her back and robbing her husband. In 1816, he and others were indicted for assaulting three men, including Alfred Huger, a member of one of the more prominent families in Charleston. Again, in 1816, he was found guilty of perjury.

According to the *Charleston Courier*, William Heyward was described as one of the leaders. Remember that there were two houses involved, the Five Mile House and the Six Mile House. After the burning of Five Mile and the removal of the undesirables of Six Mile, David Ross had been put in charge of the Six Mile House. It was apparent from Ross's statement that all the parties had gathered at Six Mile. From investigation it appears that Heyward was the proprietor of Five Mile House. A later article would refer to him as a member of the "five mile house fraternity." Although all the members were considered part of the same gang, and the terms Five Mile House gang and Six Mile House gang are synonymous and refer to the same group of people, there is a distinct division as to the identity of the inns' proprietors. The Fishers ran Six Mile, and William Heyward ran Five Mile.

On March 23, 1819, the Fishers, William Heyward and Joseph Roberts were brought up on a Writ of Habeas Corpus before sixty-five-year-old Judge Elihu Hall Bay. Judge Bay was described as a stuttering, crotchety old man who constantly repeated himself. Judge Bay indeed stuttered very badly. He once referred to a defendant's lies as "the d-d-desperate effort of every d-d-desperate d-d-desperado." Judge Bay was also mostly deaf and the evidence had to be screamed to him in order for him to even hear it. It gave the hearing the appearance of a carnival act or vaudeville comedy routine with the attorneys screaming at the judge and the old and perhaps senile judge straining over the bench to hear what was presented. In reality, it was supposed to be a hearing to establish if there was enough cause and sufficient legal authority to detain the prisoners. Judge Bay determined that there was. Bond was set, and while the Fishers returned to jail, Roberts and Heyward posted bail.

Joseph Roberts did not stay free for long. On March 25, he was rearrested for threatening the life of Frederick Schwach, a butcher. Apparently this is where LaCoste's ill-fated cow ended up, and obviously he was attempting to silence the butcher prior to trial. Roberts was not going to be taken easily; he mounted a horse and, in an attempt to escape, fled up Queen Street. Apparently unknown to Roberts, the street had been opened up to clear out the sewage drain. While riding at top speed, he and the horse fell into the open ditch. The horse's neck was broken, instantly killing the animal. It obviously took a tremendous amount of impact to break the neck of a horse. That leads one to believe that Roberts had, at minimum, suffered minor injuries to himself in the incident. Injuries or not, Joseph Roberts was rearrested and returned to jail.

Meanwhile, William Heyward's bond had been posted by Stephen Moore and Richard Heyward, according to court documents. Each man had posted $250.00 each, and after the court received the total $500.00 fine, Heyward was freed. Apparently he left the city immediately. He was scheduled to appear in court on May 10, 1819, because he had been indicted for the

William Heyward's bond order. *Courtesy South Carolina Department of Archives and History.*

assault on David Ross. William Heyward chose not to return for this hearing. In fact, if he had his way, he never would have returned to Charleston at all.

This is quite a different story from the legend that attributes the crimes to Lavinia and John Fisher only. If the authorities were correct then, there were nine male coconspirators associated with the group and another female.

The victims own statements kept in the state's archive records show no use of oleander tea, no trapdoors and no multitude of corpses, and the "victims" never were guests at all. One was part of a mob—an intruder—and the second was a man watering his horses outside of the inn.

Lavinia was not a seductress and did not use her feminine wiles on either John Peoples or David Ross unless one considers being beaten about the head and shoulders and having your head slammed through a window as seduction. Along the same lines, John Fisher never butchered either victim, and even the two bodies found within the immediate vicinity were intact except for decomposition.

Of the twelve total persons attributed to the group, only four remained in jail and actually made it before the judge in March 1819. Those persons would be John and Lavinia Fisher, the keepers of Six Mile House; William Heyward, the keeper of Five Mile House; and Joseph Roberts, the hapless horseman. The only reason Roberts was being held at this time was for his threats on the butcher, Frederick Schwach.

CHAPTER 4

The Trial

COLONIAL JUSTICE IS NOT CRIMINAL JUSTICE

On May 10, 1819, the particulars of the case were heard before a jury. This jury would be similar to what is known as a grand jury by today's standards. A true bill was passed by the jury, which means that, in their belief, sufficient probable cause existed to place the defendants on trial for the crimes in which they were accused. John and Lavinia Fisher were indicted for assault with intent to murder and also common assault on David Ross with that incident being the only crime reviewed. William Heyward had jumped bail and was on the run. Joseph Roberts was no longer considered in the proceedings. Roberts had pleaded guilty to assault in regard to the butcher and was imprisoned for one year and fined $1,000.00. James McElroy's name now resurfaces. Both Heyward and McElroy were also indicted.

From the actual court document, the jurors were identified as foreman William Hart, Luke Bowes, William Wheelen, David Murray, J.S. Packer, William Owens, I. Gespeale, William Mathews, James Fogartie, Joseph Tyler, William Brisbane, Caleb Walker, Peter Gaillard, John Davis and John Wilson. Very little is known of most of these jurors. What is known is that Mathews was a planter; Tyler was a merchant; Walker was a carpenter; Davis was a mariner; and John Wilson was the state engineer.

According to the Office of State Engineer for South Carolina, the responsibility of this office is for providing construction procurement procedures and training, approvals and assistance on state construction projects. It seems odd that a person with the responsibility of state improvement projects would be sitting on a grand jury. In January through March of that year, the *Charleston Courier* documented that John Wilson had

Attorney General Robert Hayne's indictment for crimes against David Ross. *Courtesy South Carolina Department of Archives and History.*

been involved in negotiations to improving waterway access to the city for larger steamships traveling from the North Carolina mountain passes. It was hoped that within the space of three years, ships from ten to fifteen tons may pass from the mountains of North Carolina through the Wando Canal into Charleston. According to a March 9, 1819 article, negotiations were to resume in May in regard to additional issues in the contracts and funding. It is somewhat interesting that Major John Wilson would have the time to sit upon a jury if he was involved in the negotiations, unless perhaps this case might somehow pertain to his work.

Two years later, John Wilson's name would once again surface in connection with another infamous personality in Charleston's history. He would become involved in the Denmark Vesey conspiracy. It would be Wilson's slave that infiltrated the group and brought back information regarding the plans of the violent slave revolt prior to its execution. It would be the actions of this man's slave that would save Charleston from an uprising and bloody massacre in 1822.

John and Lavinia Fisher, William Heyward (in his absence) and James McElroy were indicted for assault with intent to murder and also common assault in regard to the incident involving David Ross. The actual indictment gives us insight into the particulars of the crime they were charged with. Attorney General Robert Y. Hayne's document lists the jurors mentioned

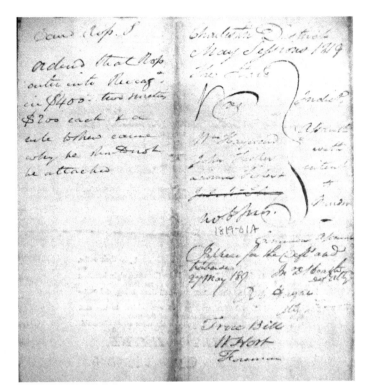

Back of indictment showing James McElroy's name scratched through and delivery of the true bill on charges. *Courtesy South Carolina Department of Archives and History.*

above and then describes the actions alleged to have been taken by the accused at the Six Mile House. The four were said to have wielded, pointed and fired a loaded weapon at David Ross with the intent to kill him. The document lists all as participants but does not tell who held the weapon and pulled the trigger. It goes on to state that Ross was mistreated, beaten, wounded and placed in great fear for his life.

On May 27, 1819, the case was heard. By now James McElroy was removed from the indictment. His name is actually scratched through on the documents—another name whittled off the original dozen associated with the gang.

With the removal of McElroy and the fact that William Heyward was still at large, this left just John and Lavinia to face the charges. Since they faced trial together as a couple and separate from any of the other members of the gang, this is why the erroneous belief arose that they acted alone. At the hearing, Attorney John Davis Heath entered a plea of not guilty for his clients, John and Lavinia Fisher.

Little is known of the Fishers' attorney, other than Heath had been appointed to the bar in 1807 and had twelve years of legal experience. He seems to have faded into obscurity after this trial.

On the other side of this case for the prosecution was the attorney general for the state of South Carolina, Robert Young Hayne. Robert Hayne had less legal experience than Heath and had been appointed to the bar in 1812.

Hayne was a free trader; in other words, he believed in a system of trade without interference from the government. This interference could come in the form of legislation or taxes, subsidies and tariffs. Hayne could exercise free trade under South Carolina's laws. This fact and other personal beliefs made him a proponent of states' rights, laws and guidelines over federal mandates; so was most of the South. He felt that such issues, including the issue of slavery, should be decided by each individual state and not the federal government. He was once quoted in one of his speeches as stating that, "The moment the federal government shall make the unhallowed attempt to interfere with the domestic concerns of the states, those states will consider themselves driven from the Union." With bold and eloquent statements such as this, Robert Hayne was also considered to be a great orator. It would take Daniel Webster, possibly the greatest orator of his time, to face him eleven years later on the floor of the Senate in regard to what is known by history as the Great Debate. This exchange would take place between the two in January and February of 1830 and would be over the very principles of the United States Constitution, the authority of the general government and the rights of the individual states.

In his current stand against federal controls and a stand he would defend in the Great Debate, Robert Hayne felt that the United States Constitution was no more than a treaty or compact between the federal government and the states, and that any state, at will, could nullify any federal law it felt contradictory to its interests. Again, this was the stance of the majority of those in power in Charleston. It was also the stance of the majority of the South, and eventually it would lead to South Carolina seceding from the Union and the beginning of the Civil War.

The fact that the Constitution and a person's constitutional rights were meaningless to Hayne and those in power like him is a key issue throughout the entire ordeal regarding the incidents at Six Mile House. From the very beginning until the absolute end of this case, one will soon learn that the United States Constitution and its amendments have very little to do with colonial justice in a Charleston courtroom. It is a lesson Attorney John Davis Heath will soon learn at the Fishers' expense.

Robert Hayne had just obtained a conviction in the Gadsden murder case, and Martin Toohey was already scheduled to face the hangman's noose the following day, May 28. Many citizens flocked to the courthouse to hear this eloquent speaker and to witness the fate of John and Lavinia Fisher.

The deck now seems to be stacked against the Fishers. They knew of the reputation of Robert Hayne and the conviction of Martin Toohey. They also knew what Toohey's fate was destined to be the following day. Heath did his best, but in the end John and Lavinia were found guilty for the crimes against David Ross. So was William Heyward in his absence. They were charged for the crimes of assault with intent to murder and common assault. They were sent back to jail to await sentencing. Remember, these facts as they will be very important in what happens later.

Less than a week later, on June 2, 1819, John and Lavinia were brought before Judge Charles Jones Colcock for sentencing. As Judge Colcock listened, John Davis Heath presented notice that a motion for a new trial would be made at the constitutional court. The constitutional court was simply a forerunner of the current court of appeals. Judge Colcock made no objections. The constitutional court would not meet again until January, so for now the Fishers were returned to the horrors of the Jail.

In the meantime, William Heyward had managed to find his way to Columbia, South Carolina. Having failed to appear at his May hearing, he was now considered a fugitive. On July 3, 1819, the *Charleston Courier* reprinted an article from the *Columbia Telescope* reporting on Heyward's capture.

Heyward, also known as Howard in this instance, was recognized and identified by a gentleman as he stayed at a hotel in Columbia. He was arrested and detained there until he could be brought back to Charleston to stand trial.

The *Columbia State Gazette* added that Heyward had with him a male and a female, both slaves. The male slave said he had been stolen by Heyward while in Charleston but had difficulty in pronouncing his master's name due to his African dialect. Since no one could interpret the name, no victim could be found and no one could prove that they were not Heyward's slaves.

Upon his arrival back to Charleston, Heyward wrote a letter to the *City Gazette*. In this letter he sought to separate himself from the Fishers. He also expounded on how he did not want to be tried with the others and used this as an excuse as to why he had not returned for trial. He also insisted that he was the one requesting to be brought back to Charleston. Most of this seems to be excuses, but what is significant is a brief excerpt regarding Fisher himself. In an effort to distance himself from John Fisher, Heyward states,

"As to Fisher having any farther correspondence with me than dealing in my store, I deny; but as a stranger, what he bought he paid for." Once again, here is indication that Heyward was the keeper of Five Mile House and that he knew Fisher as an occasional customer, not an inhabitant of Five Mile. Since business was common among the inns, this is another illustration of the separation of Heyward and Fisher as proprietors and the inns they ran.

From a total of twelve members attributed to the gang, the list had been whittled down and now there were three left facing charges. They were the keepers and proprietors of both the Five Mile House and the Six Mile House. They were husband and wife John and Lavinia Fisher and William Heyward. The final three—and no one else—were charged with the crimes against David Ross.

CHAPTER 5
The Escape

A LAST BID FOR FREEDOM

Because they were husband and wife, John and Lavinia were housed together in a single cell separate from the general population. This was an inner cell on the lowest level generally used as an isolation cell. There was little light or air flow through this cell. Conditions were horrendous.

Apparently there came an opportunity for the Fishers to be moved to another section. According to records, Lavinia pleaded with Sheriff Cleary and both she and John were moved to a less secure part of the jail used as a debtors' prison. Debtors were also held at the jail and manufactured a commodity that the jail had much use for—coffins.

The debtors' section was in an upper level of the jail where the Fishers could move freely about a larger cell. It was at this location that the Fishers were reunited with Joseph Roberts who was serving out his one-year sentence for assault on the butcher.

On the night of Monday, September 13, 1819, John Fisher and Joseph Roberts created a hole under one of the windows and lowered themselves down with blankets they had tied together. Roberts went out first, followed by Fisher. As Fisher lowered himself to the ground, the blankets broke. He fell approximately twenty feet to the ground. Lavinia could not escape. Her line to freedom had been suddenly severed. Try as he may, John could not save Lavinia that night without alerting the guards. With no alternative, John Fisher and Joseph Roberts escaped into the darkness. Fortunately for them, their escape was not noticed until the following day or they would have had the tracking dogs to contend with.

Escape may have not been the wisest of moves. The authorities of Charleston were still feeling the sting of the escape of Martin Toohey in March. Remember,

An isolation cell. *Courtesy of author.*

Original section built 1802. *Courtesy of author.*

A hole under the window in the old section is consistent with escape. *Courtesy of author.*

Toohey had been convicted of the murder of James Gadsden and hanged on May 28, the day after John and Lavinia's trial. He too had been appealed to the constitutional court and had been refused a new trial. Apparently John and Lavinia did not want to take their chances with the court and escaped when the opportunity presented itself. On the heels of the Toohey debacle, this may have sealed their fate with the powers in control of Charleston.

Martin Toohey had been sentenced to hang for the murder of James Gadsden. His brother, Michael had received a lesser charge of manslaughter and had been branded with the letter "M" in his left hand. As Martin Toohey awaited his fate his brothers, Michael and Patrick, conspired with a turnkey, or jailer, for his escape.

On March 17, 1819, Martin Toohey's shackles were discovered, left in his cell undamaged. After investigation, it was determined that a turnkey named Eery had disappeared with him, explaining the undamaged shackles. It was first thought that pirate George Clark had also escaped, but he was later discovered still inside the jail. This "misplacing" of one murderer and the escape of another aided by a turnkey had the city in an uproar.

The governor issued a $1,000 reward and a warning for the citizens to use caution and protect themselves. The Charleston Riflemen were dispatched by the governor in pursuit of the escapee and the corrupt jailer.

The group apparently came upon Martin Toohey in a swampy area outside of Charleston. Two members of the group fired at Toohey, who fled into the woods. Edward Morris, who was mounted on horseback, pursued. Toohey turned and knelt and fired a pistol at Morris. The ball passed through Morris's coat and grazed his chest. A second pistol was fired and the ball went through his sleeve. This time, before Toohey could reload either weapon, Morris caught up with the escapee and struck Toohey in the head with his sword, knocking him to the ground. Other members of the group rushed in and secured him. The wound was obviously pretty gruesome but determined to not be life threatening.

The turnkey, Eery, was captured nearby, and both were escorted back to jail. One was tied to the cart and one was placed inside it. Eery later made a confession, stating he was to have received $600, two watches and coins that were provided by the two brothers and left with a James Riley until Toohey reached safety. Since Toohey had been injured, one assumes that Eerie was the one tied to the cart and dragged behind it back to Charleston. Being dragged behind a cart and his subsequent interrogation prompted the confession.

Another interesting note in the Toohey ordeal is the fact that the Charleston Riflemen brought him back to Charleston to be tried by Attorney General Robert Young Hayne. Hayne had served in the War of 1812 and had become the captain of the Charleston Riflemen in 1814. The fact that Martin Toohey murdered someone, escaped from jail and then fired upon members of a unit his prosecutor had commanded definitely led him to a long drop attached to a short rope.

The jail authorities had a unique interrogation device known as the crane of pain. This device had the prisoners feet shackled to the floor while ropes were attached to each wrist and pulled through a pulley attached to the ceiling. The prisoner would be stretched as far as he could and when he thought he could stretch no more the guards found a way to remedy that. The prisoner then would often be left there for quite some time only to be revisited by the guards, whipped and interrogated. Once having been the deliverer of torture, it appears Mr. Eery now had become the recipient.

Now just six months after the Toohey debacle, Charleston was facing another escape.

On September 15, 1819, the *Charleston Courier* ran a brief article regarding the escape. Governor Geddes had issued a proclamation offering a $500 reward for the apprehension of John Fisher. It states that he had made his escape that Monday evening accompanied by Joseph Roberts. There is no reward mentioned for Roberts at all even though he was serving a yearlong sentence, had escaped from the jail in the past, in addition to a Georgia jail. It seems that although he seemed the most threatening to the citizens of Charleston, it was John Fisher that the governor was most interested in recovering.

Many things have been written about John Fisher and his cowardice. It has also been written that he took every opportunity to blame Lavinia for what they were accused of. In all the research that was conducted in regard to this case and the preparation of this book, one thing is certain: John Fisher was devoted to his wife and defended both her innocence and his until the very end. It is believed that John had planned to board a schooner within the Charleston harbor and sail to Cuba. He would not leave Lavinia behind in Charleston; he stayed in the area, along with Joseph Roberts, trying to devise a scheme to rescue her.

On Tuesday night following the escape, grocer William Bull was keeping late hours at his store on South Bay. He glanced outside and observed two men in the darkness paddling toward shore in a small canoe. One entered the store as the other walked off into the darkness. The customer made a few purchases, but the grocer became suspicious of him. As the man left, Bull secretly followed him and observed him crawl under an overturned boat on the wharf. Bull had a colleague monitor the situation while he left and alerted authorities.

Fisher and Roberts were located hiding under the overturned boat and were rearrested. The *Charleston Courier* reported the events on September 16, 1819: "John Fisher and Joseph Roberts who escaped from the Jail in this city on the evening of the 13th were apprehended on Tuesday night and a number of gold pieces and watches were found in their possession."

The two men were returned to jail and kept under heavy guard. Both men had the opportunity to escape and flee Charleston. They were given the opportunity, took advantage of it and did indeed escape, but yet both refused to leave Lavinia behind. The breaking of the makeshift rope had left Lavinia to the horrors of the jail, and it appears that John Fisher and Joseph Roberts had spent their brief moments of freedom amassing a bribe similar to the bribe the turnkey received in the Toohey escape. If you recall from earlier, that bribe was $600, two watches and some coins. Perhaps they intended to obtain Lavinia's release much in the same manner Toohey's brothers had obtained Toohey's release.

Whatever their plans were, the escape sealed their fate with the authorities of Charleston just four months before they were to appear in court again.

Then again, their fate may have been already predetermined before they ever reached court and that is why they chanced escape.

There was great complaining of the condition of the Old City Jail with this escape following so closely on the heels of the Toohey escape. Charleston architect Robert Mills was commissioned to create plans to reinforce and redesign the jail. His additions would be completed in 1822. Mills was perhaps one of the greatest architects of his time. He was well-known for his works in designing courthouses, jails and other buildings in South Carolina. He was known for his expertise in "fire-proofing" buildings in their designs. One of his projects in Charleston is known as the Fire-Proof Building and houses the historical records and documents of the South Carolina Historical Society. In later years, Robert Mills would design the Washington Monument, perhaps his most famous work.

With this botched escape one begins to see a different John Fisher emerge than what the legend has taught us. It shows a man desperate to save the life of his wife and his commitment to her even at the risk of his own life. Starting with their arrest in the very beginning, his devotion toward Lavinia never waivers. He was a man very dedicated to his wife. John Fisher may have been many things, but he was far from being a coward and he is not the blood thirsty butcher of legend. It is the turning point in the story on a multitude of levels.

CHAPTER 6
The Sentencing

COLONIAL JUSTICE EQUALS COLONIAL CORRUPTION

On January 17, 1820, John and Lavinia Fisher appeared before the constitutional court. The following day, the *Charleston Courier* reported that John and Lavinia Fisher were convicted of highway robbery at the last court of sessions and now had been brought before the constitutional court and received their sentencing under the law. After a motion for a new trial had been rejected and "admonitory addresses" from Judges Colcock and Bay were given, the Fishers were condemned to be hanged on Friday, February 4, 1820.

What is most notable is the fact that their charges have now been changed from what they were originally convicted of. Remember that they were charged for the crimes of assault with intent to murder and also common assault? They were indicted for those crimes, and they were convicted and sent back to jail to await sentencing. Remember that this was all for the assault on David Ross? Now, sentencing day has come, and they were now being sentenced for a different crime altogether. They were being sentenced for the highway robbery upon John Peoples.

What had transpired here? They were tried and convicted for one crime against one victim. It was appealed. Their appeal was rejected at this hearing and now, at this same hearing, they are being sentenced to death for a crime against a different victim. They were never tried or convicted of the crime in which they were now being condemned to die for.

In all the research, there is nothing to show that they were ever formally charged for the crimes against John Peoples. Now all of a sudden they are condemned to die for those crimes?

Now, if you recall in Chapter 3, they were all brought before Peoples and identified, although they were never formally charged with that crime. What happened there and why will become an issue, but we will get to that shortly. For now, let's explore another element that is as equally troubling. Our villains, the source of the most vile and despicable crimes ever to have occurred in Charleston, are beginning to appear to have been railroaded and may be the actual victims themselves.

By the time February 4 rolled around, a brief respite in the carrying out of the execution was granted. After he had received a petition from John Fisher and Lavinia Fisher, several clergy members and a number of respectable citizens "imploring an opportunity for repentance, and asking but for time to prepare to meet their God," Governor Geddes, "for these special purposes," granted a respite in the execution of their sentence until Friday, February 18, 1820.

During this time, John and Lavinia were visited by numerous clergy officials attempting to prepare their physical bodies for the execution and their souls for the judgment thereafter. One of the clergy, an elderly Baptist pastor, spent much time there. Despite his wife having died the previous year, leaving him to care for a large family, he felt called to assist the couple. His congregation was also busy building a new church that needed his attention, but he still managed to find the time to minister to the couple in prayer. This man was the Reverend Dr. Richard Furman.

Dr. Furman had led a very active life in the Baptist ministry and had greatly influenced the development of the Baptist denomination. He had been converted at the age of sixteen in 1771 because of the influence of a pastor, Joseph Reese, in the Santee area of South Carolina. By May 1774, he had been ordained and was pastor of the High Hills Baptist Church. That year he was married to Elizabeth Haynsworth. Together they had four children until her death in 1787. The distraught minister left High Hills Baptist Church that same year and found himself in Charleston as pastor of the Charleston Baptist Church. Two years later, in 1789, he would marry Dorothea Burn. Together they had thirteen children. Now she had died and Dr. Furman began to identify with the condemned couple and the agony they faced at the thoughts of not only losing each other, but the thoughts of losing their own lives.

The sixty-five-year-old pastor could also identify with John and Lavinia on another level. When he was much younger, he had volunteered for duty in the Revolutionary War only to be halted by Governor John Rutledge. Rutledge wanted Furman to plead the patriot cause to the South Carolina

Loyalists, those loyal to the crown. When Dr. Furman's efforts began to succeed on a large scale, he came to the attention of the British general lord Charles Cornwallis, who after capturing Charleston in 1780 put a bounty on Furman. Although he had never faced imprisonment, he had indeed lived with the fear of capture and hanging at the hands of the redcoats.

In life, Dr. Furman was a kind and caring pastor. Later, after his death in 1825, he would become a very controversial figure. He would later be glorified for his stand on education and an educated ministry and Furman University would eventually be founded and named for this man. He would also be vilified for his reversal on his stand in support of slavery. His work titled "Exposition of the Views of the Baptist Relative to the Coloured [*sic*] Population of the United States" in 1822 supported slavery as economically necessary and morally justified. It would become, literally, a bible in which supporters religiously and intellectually justified slavery for the next forty years and throughout the Civil War.

Dr. Furman worked hard with the Fishers in preparing their souls for what lay ahead. He found it much easier to reach John than Lavinia. When

Lavinia was more concerned with her life than her soul and put her faith in the governor's pardon more than God's mercy. *Courtesy of Kayla Orr.*

engaged with prayer, Lavinia would jump at any movement or noise by her captors. She was convinced they were coming to her with a pardon. When it proved not to be the case, Lavinia would burst into profanity laced tirades and the elderly reverend would have to start his efforts toward her salvation all over again. Dr. Furman built a strong rapport with John Fisher that would eventually lead John to address his final letter to the pastor to be read at his execution. Lavinia, on the other hand, was consumed with only one thought: a pardon. She professed her innocence and believed she would be exonerated. She also believed that the governor would not hang a woman.

There are many opinions to the reason behind the respite in the execution other than the governor's concern for the Fishers' immortal souls. One resource claims the reason for the respite was because February 4 fell during Race Week. Race Week was the most important sporting and social event of the new calendar year. A hanging just could not detract from a horse race. Beggar Girl beating Envoy and Corvisart in two out of three heats was exciting, and the competition with a hanging of a married couple would conflict. The decision was made to move the hanging to another date in order to create two separate major events to draw in crowds—and commerce—to Charleston.

Although this may have partially been the case, further research has found a possible third and more serious reason. There was question of their guilt.

Within a pamphlet printed by Nathaniel Coverly in 1820 are the first indications that another individual had admitted to the crimes. According to the pamphlet, as their execution date approached, there was a respite in execution granted by the governor, of which we are already aware. The reason Coverly gives is a man was arrested for a different crime, and as he was brought before the magistrate, he declared he was the perpetrator for the crimes in which John and Lavinia Fisher were sentenced. His confession seemed quite compelling because he was able to furnish the exact time and place of the robbery, the exact amount of money taken and several other significant elements of the crime. Apparently this information had been provided to Governor Geddes and the respite was granted. There was hope, according to Coverly, that further information might be obtained to exonerate the Fishers so they would not be executed for a crime of which they did not commit.

A letter from "G.-S." to a friend in Boston also makes claim that there was a person that came forward: "The whole city has manifested a deep interest in the fate of Fisher and his wife ever since sentence was passed upon them. The public papers have doubtless informed you of the reprieve granted them in consequence of the confession made by another person." The city hoped that this would make a difference to the condemned Fisher couple and their execution would not be carried out. The Coverly pamphlet and the letter from G.-S show a different perspective of the citizens of Charleston than what the legacy of the legend has taught us. The people of Charleston, South Carolina, supported the Fishers and even hoped their innocence could be proven.

Lavinia had also begun to receive additional support from another source—"the most fashionable ladies of Charleston." These ladies felt that the execution of a "white female" would be a reflection on all women. In other words, it would set a precedent that would now include "white women" under the umbrella of colonial law and punishment that covered everyone else. They prepared petitions for the governor; Governor Geddes avoided them at all costs.

Apparently the new reprieve did not last long, and the confession of the person that admitted his guilt did little to change things. In his pamphlet, Coverly went on to say that the man who had confessed to the crimes for which the Fishers were condemned was reexamined and his statements became contradictory. His sanity was also called into question. Perhaps the crane of pain changed his mind at confessing to the crimes. The respite was not extended and the execution was to be carried out on the appointed date.

John and Lavinia Fisher had been convicted of a crime against one man and sentenced to die for a crime against another man. This was a crime they never went to trial on and were never convicted of as far as the records reflect. We have a person coming forward—knowing he will be sentenced to die for this crime—admitting to the crime. This person was later reexamined (we have learned how colonial authorities examined their prisoners) and deemed insane. We have clergy and citizen groups standing behind the Fishers. What does the governor decide to do amid all this chaos surrounding the Fishers? Governor Geddes leaves the city to avoid the hoopla.

What had occurred painted an entirely different picture of the Fishers and what had transpired. It plants that seed that takes us into the realm of reasonable doubt. Surely a jury would have a reasonable doubt. The problem is that there was no jury. Judge Colcock and the senile Judge Bay disregarded the previous matter and deemed them guilty of another crime without a trial. They sentenced them to die for that crime.

One now begins to have a sense of uneasiness and actually disdain for what happened to the Fishers. This was exactly what the citizens of Charleston were feeling in 1820. It was a feeling of doubt in their justice system; it was a sense of corruption.

In February 1820, a question began to form in the minds of Charlestonians because of the events they were watching unfold in regard to the Fishers. That same question is now forming in your mind some 190 years later.

Could they actually have been innocent?

CHAPTER 7

The Execution

IN THE WORDS OF THOSE WHO WITNESSED IT

Behold the husband and the wife
Pay the dear forfeit of life:
In bloom of youth they meet their end,
And none can now their cause defend.
O may this sight a warning be,
To shun the paths of misery,
And when we die, O, may we prove,
The gifts of Heaven's pard'oing love.
—From a pamphlet by Nathaniel Coverly 1820

Execution.—The awful sentence of law is this day to be carried into effect upon John
Fisher, and Lavinia, his wife, who were sentenced to death, at the late sitting of the
Constitutional Court, for the crime of high-way robbery. We understand that they are to
meet their fate just without the lines, on the Meeting Street Road, between the hours of 12
and 4 o'clock.
—Charleston Courier, *Friday, February 18, 1820*

In 1834, an eyewitness recorded the events of the execution in stunning detail in an essay. The essay would be known as "Essays on Capital Punishment." Charleston attorney John Blake White never forgot what he witnessed, and some fourteen years later he included his observations within these essays.

On February 17, 1820, the eve of the Fisher's execution, Charleston attorney John Blake White found himself called to the City Jail on professional business. He accompanied the jailer to the ground cells of the jail where the jailer unlocked a large chamber. As the jailer's lantern illuminated the room, White observed that it was filled with coffins, a disassembled gibbet, sections of rope, a shovel and pickaxe and other similar instruments. The jailer examined the gibbet to assure that it was functioning properly for the events of the following day. Two appropriately sized coffins were selected and turned over to an assistant.

White continued to follow the jailer about his duties and found himself at another cell at a remote corner of the jail. The jailer repeatedly called into the cell and eventually a voice answered from within. The voice sounded like the voice of death itself manifested in the flesh. Little did he know that it actually was the voice of death.

The jailer unbarred the door, and there White observed a haggard, pale, emaciated creature slowly rising from the floor. White would write, "It stood at length erect before us, resembling more of an anatomical preparation than a true and living man...—This was the Executioner! We stood in the awful presence of a Minister of Justice and shrunk with reverential horror at his glance!"

John Blake White had met the hangman.

The hangman was a solitary individual with no family ties. He received pension from the sheriff who found it necessary to confine him to jail in an effort to sober him prior to an execution. The hangman apparently battled with the demons of the many executions he had performed for the state. His obvious weapon to confront his memories was alcohol. Apparently his only time of sobriety was when he was confined inside the jail prior to the utilization of his talents. White states the man demanded liquor repeatedly and was refused—"Thus am I served (growled he) whenever you want my work. But give me something to drink—I must have drink and I will be contented!" White also states that the hangman was reassured that after the execution, performed well, he would be furnished as much alcohol as he desired. With that a smile came upon the hangman's face for a moment and the door was once again closed and bolted, leaving this now-functioning alcoholic to plan the Fishers' execution.

The following day, White returned to the jail at the request of the newly elected sheriff, Francis G. Deliesseline. Inside the jail, he heard a minister speaking with the Fishers over their fate and their salvation. He states that loud lamentations, sighs, sobs and moans were heard from within the cell only to be followed with eerie silence and then unnerving frantic shrieks.

White retreated to the lobby to await the sheriff and the attendants and to give the condemned their privacy. There he once again encountered the hangman arranging the ropes and the nooses. He then busied himself with the calculations necessary to ensure the proper length of the ropes. Too long and the condemned would strangle to death. Too short and the condemned would be decapitated with the head being flung wildly into the spectators. Either of these events would render this a poorly performed execution and his payment of alcohol would be deprived. The hangman would not have any of that.

As White watched the executioner with a morbid curiosity, the door to the lobby opened and the Fishers were escorted in. Lavinia's eyes fell upon the hangman and she shrieked in terror. Her cry, according to White, "chilled every heart with horror."

The prisoners had provided themselves, at their own expense, loose white garments to wear over their clothing. They threw themselves into one another's arms in a farewell that was agonizing to behold.

After much pleading and resistance from Lavinia, the hangman adjusted his chords and restrained and pinioned the Fishers. The hangman was very cold and indifferent in the words of White. White further states that to depict the horrors of the moment it would take a literary master. He states that he was incapable of the words necessary to describe each minute instant in the terrible scene playing out in front of him. The hangman took charge of the couple and never left them for an instant. As White viewed the scene, he states of the hangman that "it was impossible to consider him but as the most debased and abandoned of the human race." He further states that only God could define the difference between the executioner and those he executed. There was little difference.

At this point White is now referring to the Fishers as "the unhappy victims." In contrast, he refers to the executioner as "debased." The scene playing out before him was one he never forgot and one in which he felt pity for the condemned and disgust for the man now controlling their fate. He watched the events as one would watch a cat toying with a mouse. The hangman enjoyed every second of the game in anticipation of the kill.

The Fishers descended the stairs arm in arm to a coach waiting at the prison door. The procession moved slowly to their final destination flanked by a company of cavalry. Due to the fact that a woman was being executed, an immense crowd of spectators had assembled, which was expected. This was anticipated by those in authority—thus the need for the company of cavalry. The city had become quite fond of the Fishers and a show of military might was needed to thwart any ideas from the crowd of rescuing the couple.

As the group arrived at the site, White states that he never forgot the horrible picture of despair on the face of John Fisher as the reality set in as he first set sight on the gibbet. John Fisher turned pale at the sight. His eyes involuntarily closed and a tremor shook his entire body. As he recovered inside the carriage, he drew Lavinia to him in a convulsive grasp. In a few seconds, he looked up and nerved himself for the execution.

The Fishers and the executioner exited the carriage. As John climbed the scaffold, he looked mournfully out at the immense crowd and back at his wife. Lavinia refused to mount the scaffold. Neither persuasion nor threats moved her, and the constables were forced to drag her to the stand. She adamantly refused to believe she was destined to hang. She called to the crowd to rescue her and stretched forth her trembling arms as far as her restraints would allow and began imploring their pity. One minute Lavinia would profess

"The Hanging of Lavinia Fisher" by artist David Gobel.

her innocence and her belief that a woman should not be hanged. She then began to blaspheme, curse and stomp and damned Governor Geddes to hell for condemning a woman to hang. Silence hung over the crowd only to be repeatedly broken by Lavinia's cycle of appalling shrieks, profanity laced curses and pitiful pleas.

On the gallows, John turned to his wife and tenderly pleaded with her to make peace with God. She continued to be defiant. In response to the efforts of Reverend Joseph Galluchat to lead her to repentance and prepare her for death, Lavinia spoke the words that would galvanize her in Charleston history and infamy. "Cease! I will have none of it. Save your words for others that want them. But if you have a message you want to send to Hell, give it to me; I'll carry it."

Dr. Irving and Mrs. Stoney were also witnesses to the execution and would later state in regard to Lavinia that "Her ravings were terrible and her husband's efforts to soothe her and point her to repentance were most touching."

Another witness, known only as G.-S. would later write to a friend that John Fisher had tried to "console his wife, and encourage her to meet death with fortitude, and a humble reliance on the goodness and mercy of Heaven." She seemed to heed his pleas but exhibited a great unwillingness to die. He believed that she held onto hope that the state would not execute a woman.

Indeed Lavinia believed she would be pardoned. The sheriff inadvertently examined a written document in the presence of the Fishers. Lavinia grasped at the belief that it was the pardon she knew would be granted. The sheriff realized his error and refolded the document as Lavinia was about to leap from the platform in anticipation of her freedom. The sheriff, in a sober and impressive voice, assured Lavinia that her hopes in a pardon were groundless and that she would not receive one. He advised her that her moments were few and that she was indeed going to die. The words were like electricity through Lavinia, and the reality of the moment came crashing in. Her ravings stopped, and she began to call upon heaven to have mercy upon her and allow her to live. In tremendous panic and conflict, she continued to plea and cry out to God. In her final moments, she made her peace.

G.-S. states that a clergyman addressing God on behalf of the Fishers was so overcome with emotion that he could hardly speak. He observed tears on the cheeks of the pastor and described him as having been overcome by the heart-rending scene. From research, this is believed to have been Dr. Furman.

John Fisher addressed the crowd. According to the witness, G.-S., Fisher begged forgiveness of those he had ever offended and he forgave his accusers. He also proclaimed his and Lavinia's innocence.

In a letter addressed to the attending reverend and dated the day of his execution, John wrote:

> *Charleston Gaol. Feb. 18*
>
> *Rev. and Dear sir,*
>
> *The appointed day has arrived—the moment soon to come, which will finish my earthly career; and it behooves me, for the last time, to address you and the Rev. Gentlemen associated in your pious care.*
>
> *For your exertions in explaining the mystery of our Holy Religion, and the merits of our dear Redeemer; for pious sympathy, and benevolent regards as concerns our immortal souls, accept Sir, for yourself, and them, the last benediction of the unfortunate—God, in His infinite mercy, reward you all.*
>
> *In a few moments, and the world to me shall have passed away—before the Throne of the Eternal Majesty of Heaven I must stand—shall then, at this dreadful hour, my convulsed, agitated lips, still proclaim a falsehood? No! then by that Awful Majesty I swear, I am innocent. May the Redeemer of the World plead for those who have sworn away my life.*
>
> *To the unfortunate, the voice of condolence is sweet, the language of commiseration is delightful; the feelings I have experienced in the society of Mr._____; a stranger; he rejected not our prayer, unknown, he shut not his ear to our supplication, he has alleviated our sorrows: may God bless him. He has wept with us: May Angels rejoice with him at a Throne of Glory.*
>
> *Enclosed, Sir is a key that secretes my little all; Give it him, and say for me, as he deserted me not while living, I hope he will discharge my last request. Now my property is to be disposed of, he will find explained in a paper within my trunk, to which is attached a Schedule of the whole. I only wish him to see it removed to a place of safety, until to whom it is given shall call for it. The hour is come.*
>
> *Farewell, Sir, Farewell!*
>
> *John Fisher*

This letter was read aloud to the crowd. The recipient's name was left blank at its reading and all subsequent referrals to it also have the name redacted. Most speculate it was Reverend Furman, but exactly who it was and exactly what John Fisher left behind remains unknown. It is believed the name was left out to protect the recipient of the letter until after John Fisher's belongings were dispersed as Fisher wanted.

The True Story of John and Lavinia Fisher

Both the *Charleston Courier* and the *Charleston Gazette* would also carry the story of John Fisher's proclamation of innocence. The *Gazette* even published his letter.

> *A letter published below, was there read, by a Rev. Clergyman to whom he had addressed it yesterday, protesting his innocence—to which he added a short address to the same purport, but accusing some persons of having been instrumental in causing him to suffer for a crime of which he was not guilty. He asked pardon of the spectators for any wrong or injury he might have done them.*

The Fisher letter's proclamation of innocence also had an effect on G.-S. He writes:

> *It is indeed a pathetic letter, and if he has there told the truth, which I can scarcely doubt, I pray that God may have mercy on his accusers. The opinions of a jury generally lean to the side of justice, but like all men else, they are liable to be mistaken. I would charitably hope, that in the case of Fisher and his wife, they have been mistaken; for the strongest circumstantial evidence, should be required, in a case of life and death to warrant the conviction of the accused party, and I can scarcely believe that a man would leave the world with the solemn declaration of innocence of the crime for which he suffered, on his lips, if he was in fact and in deed, the perpetrator of it.*

Obviously this witness had his doubts to the guilt of the Fishers.

While all this was occurring, Attorney John Blake White noted that the hangman was poised on a ladder, "hovering like a vampire" over the couple. He was engaged in some last-minute adjustment of the ropes.

G.-S. states that in her last moments, Lavinia looked out at the multitude gathered. He states that he was in a few yards of the scaffold and had a fair view of her countenance at the end. He stated that he believed that grief, not guilt, was depicted upon her face. He stated that she seemed filled with woe and burdened with sorrow. As he watched, serenity seemed to descend upon her and a smile came upon her face in contrast to the proceedings surrounding her. "She look'd [sic] like patience on a monument, Smiling at grief." Perhaps she had come to the realization that her death was inevitable and God granted her peace. More so perhaps she was in a state of shock and disbelief and had succumbed to its effects on her mind.

The hangman descended and placed the caps over the Fishers' faces. The pair stood trembling upon the platform for a brief moment longer. A private signal was given by the sheriff and the platform gave way. The couple dropped and all was quiet and still except for their loose white garments fluttering on the breeze.

In the final portion of his letter regarding the execution, G.-S. would write, "the wretched sufferers have gone to that tribunal from whence there is no appeal, and there their guilt or innocence will plainly appear. Human judgement [sic] will be of no further as regards their conduct, for there they will be sure to meet with JUSTICE."

The following day the *Charleston Courier* reported on the execution. It reported that, at a little past 2 o'clock in the afternoon, the husband and wife embraced each other up on the platform for the last time. The signal was given and the drop fell. Lavinia died without a struggle or a groan, but it was some minutes before John expired and ceased to struggle. After hanging the usual time, their bodies were taken down and taken to Potter's Field, where they were buried. The reporter's final comments were that "May the awful example strike deep into their hearts; and may it have the effect intended, by deterring others from pursuing those vicious paths which end in infamy and death."

John Fisher was only twenty-nine years old; Lavinia was just twenty-eight.

On June 6, 1820, William Heyward was denied a new trial at the constitutional court and sentenced to death by Judge Gantt. His execution was to take place on June 30, 1820, but he was also given a respite by the governor to make his peace with God. On August 11, 1820, at 1:00 p.m., William Heyward was also hanged. He too went to his death proclaiming his innocence. Reverend Mund attended Heyward's last moments, and the event was witnessed by several hundred spectators.

Despite having a sordid past, Heyward did have a family. William Heyward left behind a wife and three small children, all under the age of four.

CHAPTER 8
The Method

DEATH BY HANGING

It has indeed been said that "marriage, like hanging, goes by destiny;" but the destiny, I conceive is the only point of similitude between the two predicaments.
—The Autobiography of Jack Ketch, *1835*

If death is the common destiny between marriage and hanging, then John and Lavinia Fisher are the perfect examples of that common destiny. John "Jack" Ketch was an English executioner used by King Charles II in the late 1600s. He had become famous because of the way he had performed his duties. He also became infamous for the same reason. Executions were supposed to be quick and merciful. During one beheading in 1683, Ketch had to make five strokes with his axe and then finally use a knife to remove the head of the person being executed. The condemned suffered greatly. Although Ketch made several apologies and stated that he had been interrupted while taking aim, it was rumored that Ketch had acted more sadistically than clumsily. Regardless of his fame or his infamy, his name lived on.

As one could easily surmise, the executioner was probably not a well-liked individual. His identity was concealed with a mask while he carried out his grisly tasks. It was the name, Jack Ketch, given and used to identify all executioners to protect their true identity. It was a name that Attorney John Blake White used repeatedly to identify the hangman in his essay.

As a form of execution five different types of methods were developed: suspension, the short drop, the standard drop, the long drop and a mechanized form of hanging known as the upright jerker. Each of these had their pluses and their setbacks.

Suspension hanging was exactly as it sounds. A person was tied to the rope, and the gallows allowed the condemned to be raised upward and suspended. This was a slow and agonizing death by strangulation.

The short drop was done by placing a fixed rope around the condemned's neck and placing them on a cart, horse or even a stool and having that said item pulled out from underneath. Again this usually resulted in a death by strangulation.

The standard drop was used pretty much as the primary method during the nineteenth century. It involved a standard drop of between four and six feet. The gallows were equipped with a trap door, and as the door fell open, the condemned dropped the standard distance. This was usually sufficient to break the condemned's neck and was a more "humane" and immediate death in most cases. Remember that this was a "standard." The executioner did not account for variations in weight or height. The "standard" person may drop and have his neck immediately broken. A smaller person may drop and strangle to death. A heavy person of three hundred pounds or more may drop and be totally decapitated due to his own weight, inertia and gravity. Things often got messy with this form, but it was the most used. It is the type that was used on John Fisher, Lavinia Fisher and William Hayward.

The long drop and the upright jerker came much later. The long drop was developed as a method to improve upon the standard drop. In this form, a person's individual height and weight were taken into account in order to determine how much fall would be sufficient to render a broken neck and not a decapitation. Unfortunately, this did not come about until 1872.

The upright jerker was a mechanized form of hanging used to make things a little more efficient than the others. A machine dropped a weight attached to one end of the rope while the other was tied around the condemned's neck. Of course the machine did not take into account height and weight. If you were extremely tiny it sent you flying. If you were obese it just sent your head flying. If you were extremely obese it may just drag you slowly upward and allow you to remain hanging, suspended, until you strangled to death.

By the time the upright jerker was created and being used, it was more of an issue of quantity than quality in executions. It was used in the Old City Jail in Charleston and was a favorite—messy as it was.

Regardless of the method of hanging, prisoners were left dangling at the end of the rope for a minimum of one hour. This was the usual amount of time allotted to make sure the condemned was dead. If a message was being sent to the community, they were often left hanging longer so more people would have the opportunity to view them.

There were also several knots used, but the most used was the hangman's knot or noose knot. It was considered the most efficient because the manner in which it was tied made the knot very large. The standard was to place the knot under the left ear and as the condemned reached the end of the drop the jerk against the large knot was sufficient to break the neck. If the hangman was sadistic or held a grudge, he could position the knot a little to the left or right and the neck would not break. The condemned would die a slow death of strangulation. This would be a good reason not to say anything that might anger your executioner. You may literally come to the end of your rope and find the knot in the wrong place.

In White's recollection of the execution, it is quite obvious that the hangman had been quite the experienced executioner. By the amount of alcohol he craved, it was obvious the weight of those many executions did not rest well upon him. Regardless, this was obviously not his first execution.

White also noted that as John Fisher was making his proclamation of innocence and claims against those who condemned him, the hangman was on the ladder engaged in working with the ropes.

The noose traditionally has thirteen twists. If a person was "lucky," he may get nine, one twist for each life, just like a cat. *Courtesy of Kayla Orr.*

In the account of the execution in the *Charleston Courier*, it states in regard to Lavinia that "She died without a struggle or a groan." Obviously the hangman showed mercy on Lavinia and the standard drop and hangman's knot sufficiently broke her neck.

The *Charleston Courier* account in regards to John Fisher's death was not as "pleasant": "it was some minutes before he expired and ceased to struggle." For whatever the reason, John Fisher's neck did not break. Some accounts say he struggled for up to seventeen minutes before dying. Obviously the hangman did not position the knot appropriately. Lavinia suffered a quick and immediate execution with the snap of her neck; John slowly suffered and died of strangulation at the end of a rope.

Maybe it was something in the words he said. Remember, in the end, he swore his innocence and accused others. "I swear, I am innocent. May the Redeemer of the World plead for those who have sworn away my life."

Lavinia Fisher is said to have been the first woman executed in this country. Actually many women were executed in the Salem Witch trials. This is where the confusion of Lavinia having been a witch came from. There are no indications that she was.

Many have stated that the fact that she used oleander to poison her victims points to the fact she was Wiccan and therefore a witch since Wiccans use herbs and flowers in their "potions." There are several problems with that theory. First of all, as we have found, there is no documentation that she used oleander as a poison on anyone. That is a complete fabrication. Second, practically everyone used herbs back then as remedies, making the entire country Wiccan in one form or another. Third, and most important, the Wiccan Code says to harm no one. The Wiccan Rede states, "These Eight words the Rede fulfill: An Ye Harm None, Do what ye Will." That excludes anyone who would use oleander to murder another person. There is no proof Lavinia Fisher was Wiccan or a witch.

Lavinia Fisher is also said to have been the first woman hanged for murder within the United States. Actually, Margaret Hatch was hanged on June 24, 1633, for murdering her own child in Virginia. Mrs. Hatch tried to avoid her hanging by claiming pregnancy. A group of midwives was gathered together and a "Jury of Matrons" was organized. The defendant was determined not to be pregnant and subsequently hanged. Margaret Hatch's execution precedes Lavinia Fisher by 187 years.

CHAPTER 9

The Allegations

COLONIAL JUSTICE VERSUS CRIMINAL JUSTICE

Now the fact that all three proclaimed their innocence all the way to the gallows and the fact that John Fisher blamed someone is an intriguing notion. The next two chapters will explore the possibility that the three were telling the truth. It will also explore what others may have had to gain by framing them.

We have already seen that there were problems in the trials and in the colonial justice system as a whole. Now let's take an opportunity to look at a few more issues. Let's start with physical identification.

Lavinia Fisher was said to be gorgeous. That is how she has lived on in legend. By the time she spent a year in jail and reached the gallows, she was described as woe worn and not a handsome woman. In David Ross's statement, he identified Lavinia but also states there was a second woman involved in his assault, quite possibly Jane Howard, the other female arrested in Colonel Cleary's raid. In John Peoples's statement, he was attacked by "a tall, stout woman." This was two hours after the Ross assault. Remember that he did not know any of his assailants. When Cleary arrived the following day, he arrested both Lavinia and Jane Howard. Could Jane Howard have been the tall, stout woman that assaulted John Peoples? Surely if Lavinia was as beautiful as was said then that would have been an identifier.

John Fisher was twenty-eight years of age. He was described as six feet tall, tall, slim, fair-skinned with dark hair and eyes. In one account, he was said to be knock-kneed.

In the 1800s, diseases such as rickets were common. We now know that left untreated this disease can cause the legs to turn inward to where the knees bend toward each other, and in severe cases, touch. In some cases being knock-kneed is hereditary. Braces can be used to correct these deformities, but they were not available then.

Knock-kneed adults are more susceptible to injury. Since they have lived with the problem most of their lives without treatment, they would have developed osteoarthritis. In severe cases, the person may have even had trouble walking. So our notorious, vicious murderer and butcher may have been handicapped. If this was indeed an identifying characteristic, wouldn't Peoples have used it as a descriptor?

Without knowing the suspects by name, how did John Peoples identify them then? Well that actually ties in directly with whom John Fisher was accusing.

In the previous chapter, you read many accounts of the execution of the Fishers. There is record that John Fisher publicly blamed someone for the couple being wrongly accused. The *Charleston Gazette* gives record that prior to his execution, John Fisher protested his innocence and made that claim.

In his final letter, read moments before his execution, John Fisher states that in mere moments he will be standing before God. Even in that final judgment he will profess his innocence and indeed be found innocent before the throne of God. In his address he also gives reference to his accusers, "May the Redeemer of the World plead for those who have sworn away my life."

Who was John Fisher accusing and what were the accusations? Those questions can be answered in a series of letters printed in the *Charleston Courier* on February 22, 1820.

> *To the Editor of the* Courier.
>
> *Sir,—A Bench Warrant, against a certain gang of highway robbers, who had infested the neighborhood of the Six-Mile House, having been put into my hands some time ago, by the Attorney General; and the Governor of the State having particularly requested me to attend to the execution of the same; I went, accompanied by a vast number of the citizens of Charleston and its precincts, to execute the unpleasant duty assigned under the authority aforesaid; and succeeded in taking, among others, the criminals who have lately suffered the penalty of the law. Fisher, one of the principal leaders of the gang, having declared under the gallows, as I understand, that "Colonel Cleary called him and the other prisoners in gaol [sic], by name, to Peoples, the countryman, and prosecutor, whom they had robbed and severely beaten, so as to enable him (Peoples) to identify the said Fisher, and others—and that his (Fisher's) blood was on Colonel Cleary's hands;"— in order to remove improper impressions, which some persons might be*

disposed to attach to the expressions of a dying culprit, I have, by advice of several friends, been induced to request you to give publicity to the following questions, put by me to the gentlemen whose names are subscribed to the answer subjoined, and whose respectability is well known to the people of this community.

I know not who was behind the curtain, and prompted or advised this calumny; but I do aver, that from no person have I ever received more general and repeated expressions of gratitude than from this unfortunate man, who continued to do so, even to the very moment that I gave up the office, but whose subsequent conduct proves that the fear of punishment does not always bring about the work of reformation.

I am, respectfully, Yours,

N.G. Cleary

It appears that the sheriff, Colonel Nathaniel Greene Cleary, is the person that John Fisher accused. Fisher accused Cleary of identifying them to Peoples by name so that Peoples could identify them as his assailants and robbers. John Peoples was from Georgia and would not have known any of these persons by name. It is kind of interesting that, if you recall back in Chapter 3, there was a handwritten list of names of the Six Mile Housemen in a completely different handwriting than the actual statement of Peoples. Apparently John Peoples was concealed behind a curtain and watched as each person was brought down before him to be identified. John Fisher claims that Sheriff Cleary verbally named him and the others Peoples identified. This is interesting because he did not know the names, but a list of names including the Fishers had been provided to him on his statement. This makes John Fisher's claim extremely plausible.

In a second letter, Cleary addresses the issues of the accusations.

To Col. Gordon, Archibald Lord, N. Slawson, and others

Saturday Morning, Feb. 19,

GENTLEMEN,

As you were present with me and many others, when I took Mr. Peoples to the gaol [sic] for the purpose of identifying the prisoners taken up by me at the six mile house, I will thank you to answer the following questions:—

1. Did I, or not, direct the gaoler [sic] to bring down the prisoners, one at a time, and were they not so brought down?

2. Did I, or not, call the name of Fisher, or any other prisoner, after he or they were so brought down and before he or they were identified by Peoples?

3. Did not Peoples promptly and unhesitatingly identify Fisher?

4. Was there any the slightest act on my part which would, in your opinion, have led you to think that I had used any means or devised any plan by which Peoples could have led to identify Fisher?

5. Was there not most perfect circumspection used by me in bringing the prisoners down before Peoples, and what is your opinion of my conduct upon that occasion?

6. How many citizens or others, do you think were present at the time Peoples identified the said prisoners? I am, very respectfully, your obedient servant,

N.G. Cleary

The third letter in the series contains the responses to Cleary's inquiries.

To Colonel N. G. Cleary,

Sunday, Feb. 20, 1820

Dear Sir,—We received your letter, and with pleasure answer the questions therein contained.

1ˢᵗ question. We answer—You did so direct, and they were accordingly brought down upon the lower floor.

2d. You did not call the name Fisher, or any other name.

3d. He did immediately identify Fisher and his wife, and Heyward and others.

4ᵗʰ. There was no act on your part which could justify even a suspicion upon the occasion. You remained down stairs; were extremely cautious in the manner in which the prisoners were brought before Peoples.

5ᵗʰ. There was the utmost possible circumspection used by you upon the occasion, and you conducted the matter with great caution and humanity. You never once called the name of fisher, or any other prisoner, but designated them by the general term of __Prisoner.__ Your conduct upon the occasion was in our opinion perfectly humane, correct and honorable.

6ᵗʰ. About twenty or thirty persons were present on the occasion.

J.G. La Roche,

J. Smith Darrell,

Nath'l Slawson,

T.J. Horsey,

Sam'l. Wilson, Jun.

And'w. M'Dowall,

A.B. Lord,

The True Story of John and Lavinia Fisher

W.E. Hill,
John Gordon,
Sam'l. K. Cowing
R.B. Lawton,
Subscribed and severally sworn before Samuel Richards, J.H. Mitchell,
and several other Justices.

Why would anyone convicted to die, knowing it was inevitable, not admit to what they had done? There are many instances of death row inmates being convicted of a capital offense crime and admitting to others to clear their conscious prior to execution. Why wouldn't John Fisher? Better yet, why wouldn't Lavinia Fisher or William Heyward? All three went to the gallows proclaiming their innocence. What reasoning would anyone have to frame the Fishers and Heyward and execute them?

Back in the very beginning, you will recall that the initial raids on Five Mile House and Six Mile House were conducted by a lynch mob with no legal authority. These men were a group acting under the guise of the Lynch's Law that held no true legal authority. In the articles it states that they acted on the authority of the owner's of the properties. David Ross was placed into possession of the house by the owner according to the *Charleston Courier* article. This shows that there was a definite land dispute. The Fishers were said to have ran Six Mile House since 1814 so had apparently occupied this property for five years. Remember that one of the key retributions under Lynch's Law was the seizure of property. The lynch mob seized Six Mile House and left Ross there.

The article stated that this lynch mob left Charleston in regard to a series of robberies upon defenseless travelers. It goes on to state that, "As they could not be identified, and thereby brought to punishment it was determined, by a number of citizens, to break them up." If the robbers could not be identified, then how could this mob identify the inhabitants of both of these Inns as the robbers in question?

In 1791, twenty-eight years prior to the events of this book, the Bill of Rights was passed. Within the Bill of Rights, the Fourth Amendment to the United Sates Constitution guarantees the right against unreasonable search and seizure. Now imagine if you will, William Heyward sitting at Five Mile House when a mob rides up and orders him to vacate his home. He and the other occupants refuse, and perhaps one of them is killed, which would account for the freshly buried male body the coroner discovered several days after the raid. The place is then set on fire. Seems like an unreasonable search and seizure.

Immediately after that, the mob proceeds to Six Mile House and conveys the same orders. This time the residents flee, and David Ross is left by the mob to take control of the house. The next morning the occupants returned with William Heyward, a man that just had all his property burned, to Six Mile House. They find Ross inside and an altercation ensues as they forcefully remove Ross, who has no lawfully authority to be there in the first place. Ross states they fired at him. The Second Amendment, also part of the Bill of Rights, gave them the right to bear arms. They had a right to protect their home and property from a legitimate threat. Their neighbor's home had been seized by armed men and burned to the ground; their home had been seized by armed men; and they had returned home to find it occupied by one of their assailants. They took action and removed him. It is a legitimate and valid argument.

Perhaps it is even one that John Heath had used. Remember that Heath was the Fishers' attorney. In the initial trial, he lost to Attorney General Robert Hayne. Again remember that Hayne was an advocate of states' laws preempting federal laws. Heath could not win on that level, so when he lost, he appealed to the constitutional court.

It is purely speculation, but this may have been the argument many believe Heath would have presented for the Ross case. This is perhaps why this case was thrown out, and the judges took the John Peoples case and ruled summarily on it. By doing so they then violated the most important right within the Bill of Rights as far as the Fishers are concerned: the Sixth Amendment right to a trial by jury. Remember that these constitutional rights had existed for twenty-eight years prior to the incident, and that the Fishers and Heyward were entitled to these rights. It did not happen. Then again, this was colonial justice and not criminal justice.

When David Ross fled Six Mile House, he returned to Charleston. He reported his assault to the sheriff. Now remember that the lynch mob rode out to these locations because of robberies. Even while David Ross was being assaulted, no one robbed him. He was not allowed to retrieve items left inside, but no one demanded items from him. Seems kind of odd that if these persons made their living robbing people, why did they not empty Ross's pockets? They were armed and could very easily have done it if they were indeed robbers. It is a very curious point that points back to residents defending their property.

What happens next is also curious. John Peoples shows up to water his horses two hours later. One finds it odd that Peoples had not heard of the events of the preceding evening and did not know what had occurred at Six

Mile House or even the burning of Five Mile House. Why did he not stop at the Four Mile House to water his horses? He had to pass it. He also had to pass the burning remains of Five Mile House, which should have made him curious. It does seem suspicious.

Peoples stopped at Six Mile House and was accosted and robbed. He then returned to Charleston, and Colonel Cleary had a robbery to act upon. This robbery justified the actions of the mob being there. Colonel Cleary, the sheriff, could now ride in, make arrests, look like a hero and justify the lynch mob.

This takes us back to John Fisher's accusations toward the good sheriff. What did Cleary have to gain if John Fisher's accusations were true? A brief advertisement in the *Charleston Courier* on June 22, 1819, gives a little insight.

The sheriff was up for reelection.

CHAPTER 10

Power and Greed

POLITICS AT ITS BEST

After the raid on the two inns, Colonel Cleary had a golden opportunity to become the hero of Charleston and sweep the election. Up until now he had several robberies in the area, but no one could identify the culprits. He had Ross being assaulted and now Peoples was victimized. With mob justice having just occurred, it obviously showed a lack of confidence in Cleary's abilities. He was pretty much obligated to act. If he did not, he could lose the election. With these victims he had an opportunity to "clean-up" Charleston. After all, he was the sheriff, and Charleston needed a good spring cleaning. The governor would bestow his blessings because the city was to be visited by the president in just under two months. Cleary could incarcerate anyone he felt was a threat.

As stated in the second chapter, the city of Charleston was in continuous competition with Savannah. Sailing ships were slowly becoming obsolete and steamships were being developed. President James Monroe was making a Southern tour, and in the beginning of April, he was in Virginia with several of his military advisers and his secretary of war to inspect Burrill's Bay, a site contemplated to be a grand naval depot. He was also inspecting several steam-powered vessels. The president's tour would take him onto Savannah via steam vessel. Charleston was also a point of interest for the president, and he would be in Charleston by the end of April. One could be quite certain that the governor did not want the embarrassment of robberies or armed lynch mobs to interfere with the president's visit. He wanted the president's visit to be unimpeded. He also wanted that naval base in Charleston.

Many of the gang had previously experienced colonial justice, had met the sheriff and spent time in the City Jail. They were not unknown to him. It is quite possible that Colonel Cleary used this opportunity to "round up all the usual suspects" as the saying goes. He could clean the streets up prior to the presidential visit, make the governor happy and win the city's voters. That is one explanation of why there were twelve criminals named to be affiliated with the gang, with ten actually arrested, four actually prosecuted and three hanged. Cleary saw an opportunity and took it. At least that's what he had to gain.

If this is what transpired, apparently he did not gain as much popularity as he thought. On January 11, 1820, an editorial appeared in the *Charleston Courier* addressed to the voters. In this editorial, the writer—the Republican elector, as he called himself—writes that Cleary had been preceded by his father and for the past eight years they had gained a monopoly on the Office of Sheriff in Charleston. The writer further alludes to Cleary's inability to continue functioning as sheriff and endorses candidate Francis G. Deliesseline.

Apparently this voter was not happy with the reign of Colonel Cleary and he was not the only one who felt this way. Francis G. Deliesseline was elected sheriff. Nathaniel Greene Cleary did not go quietly. He protested the election results and the margin of thirty-six votes. The January 14, 1820 *Charleston Courier* showed the results of the polls: Deliesseline, 1,068; Cleary, 1,032; Laval, 255; Adams, 73; Bennett, 45; Ker, 20; and Sykes, 7. By January 25, hearings had been held, and it was determined that Francis G. Deliesseline had indeed been elected sheriff.

The reign of the Cleary family, apparently not a favorable one according to the Republican elector, had come to an end—at least for four years.

On the very first day of 1820, the *Charleston Courier* ran an article regarding notification of the election of sheriff. It advised the citizens of the places to vote, and it also advises them of the qualifications. In order to vote in the election for sheriff, one of the following qualifications stands out.

> *Every free White Man, of the age of twenty-one years (Paupers and Non-Commissioned Officers and Private Soldiers of the Army of the United States excepted) being a citizen of this State, and having resided therein two years previous to the day of the Election, and who hath a freehold of 50 acres of Land, or a Town Lot, of which he hath legally seized and possessed, at least six months before such Election.*

The Six Mile House was seized February 18, 1819, along with its inhabitants. The Five Mile House was seized the same night but the inhabitant was not in custody until July 1819, exactly six months prior to the election. If the properties were seized, then the "owners" could vote.

No one believes that the properties were seized so Cleary could obtain two votes—that is a little ridiculous. The point is that property, during that time, was seized from others. The definition of seize is to take by force. That is what the lynch mob did. The mob allegedly seized the Five Mile House and Six Mile House with local owners' consent, but yet they burned both inns to the ground. No one would want their homes burned to the ground, especially when they have to resort to armed force to seize it. Yet this is what is said to have occurred. According to the *Charleston Courier* article, one must "legally" seize and possess the property for six months. Now what are the standards for seizing a property you might ask? If a property was vacant and uncontested for one year, that property could be purchased for the amount of the back taxes. A person interested in that property could move in and take possession. Obviously the lands were disputed or Ross would never have been placed in Six Mile House to guard it for the "owner."

In order to seize the Six Mile House, it had to be unoccupied and uncontested for one year. What better way to keep someone from contesting than to incarcerate them or their relatives. John and Lavinia Fisher were incarcerated on February 18, 1819. They were executed on February 18, 1820. Exactly one year to the date.

This would also explain why William Heyward was not executed on the same day as the Fishers. It was puzzling as to why he was not hanged on that date along with his colleagues in crime. Remember that he had fled to Columbia, South Carolina, and was not located and rearrested until July. He was found guilty in his absence and was actually in Charleston and could have been brought before the January hearing of the constitutional court along with the Fishers if his case was appealed. He was not, and it was not until June that his appeal was denied before that session of the constitutional court. He was executed in August of the following year. This was one year and a few weeks since his incarceration. That would have given persons interested in the Five Mile House property their year.

This brings up some valid issues and additional motive. After all, anyone with a monopoly on the inns would fair very well. Also the elimination of the Five Mile House and Six Mile House by fire would have obviously diverted any future customers to the remaining inns. This is one theory.

Could John and Lavinia Fisher and William Heyward have been the victims of a land dispute and swindle? Is that farfetched? Maybe not. One of the most prominent figures involved in this case—and probably the least most suspected—was involved in one of the earliest land scams in Florida history. In fact, this could very well be the key to the whole ordeal.

CHAPTER 11

Land Swindling

THE KEYS MAY BE KEY

The president of the United States was set to arrive in Charleston in April 1819. The governor pulled out all stops, and the president was met with an impressive display of Charleston's defensive forces. Not only was the president met and escorted by several cavalry brigades, he was also treated to a tour of the forts in the harbor. The steamboat *Charleston* escorted the president, who was accompanied by a band, other officials and select members of Charleston society. Passing the cutter *Gallatin* in the harbor, President Monroe was greeted by a twenty-one gun salute that was repeated by Castle Pinckney, Fort Johnson and Fort Moultrie upon the landing of the party. A large balloon was supposed to ascend greeting the president from the city square but high winds kept it from being inflated. This was compensated for by the fine fireworks display in the Orphan House enclosure and a very elegant dinner in his honor. The following morning, the president toured the city's defenses at the Lines, had a large breakfast with select society and continued the day, which ended with a concert and ball in his honor at the hall of the South Carolina Society on Meeting Street.

The president was wined and dined by Governor Geddes, and it was not by coincidence that the military might of Charleston was a key issue to impress the president. Governor John Geddes wanted that naval base for Charleston. For a city struggling with a dying economy, Geddes spared no expense. In fact, the balloon display attempted again at the president's exit from the city. The Messengers, Alexander and Valente, set off another balloon and this time it filled and ascended splendidly. As things for the grand display were looking up, the balloon touched one of the support posts, turned on its side and caught fire. As it passed over a small portion of the city, it burst into flames and fell from the sky in a burning mass.

It seems quite ironic that the Six Mile House and Five Mile House Properties were seized two months before his visit, the buildings razed and the owners incarcerated. This property was ideal for naval facilities and had just become available at the time of the president's arrival.

Governor John Geddes always gives one the impression that he was a man who was never satisfied with his current status. He always seemed to be planning his next move in life. In 1797, he was admitted to the bar in Charleston. He was an active member of the South Carolina militia as a cavalry major and later as a major general.

In 1808, he was elected to the South Carolina House of Representatives where he spent two of his years as speaker of the House. From there he moved to the Senate in 1816, and in 1818, he was appointed governor of the state by the General Assembly. He remained there until 1820. At this point he was a brigadier general of the militia. He later was mayor of Charleston from 1824 to 1825.

John Geddes was not one to let others interfere with his goals. In his campaign for mayor of Charleston—one of many positions he held in Charleston—he felt that his honor had been insulted by rival Edward Simons. Geddes challenged Simons to a duel in order to settle the matter and restore his honor. In duels of that time, a second was usually named and the duty of the second was to resolve the dispute prior to actual engagement in the duel. Once the duel began, it could only be ended once honor was restored to the insulted. Usually that meant the death of at least one of the parties involved.

John Geddes picked his son Thomas as his second. The second's duties were to choose the weapons to be used and the place for the duel. A second could also take the place of the principal party and exchange shots. Thomas Geddes stood in place of his father while Simons opted to settle matters himself. John Geddes made his son take his place and risk death for his honor over an insult.

A duel was basically a series of opportunities for a party to back down. Duels were held in rounds. With each round each party had an opportunity to withdraw the insult and apologize or admit the insulting party was correct. This was not the case with Geddes and Simons. Simons had an opportunity to withdraw his insult; he chose not to. John Geddes had an opportunity to withdraw to save his son; he chose not to do so. His honor was much more important than the life of his child.

Four rounds had passed between the men without the matter being resolved or blood being drawn. With each round the men drew closer and so did their aim. The projectiles moved in closer to the participants. Most duels were considered cowardly displays that dishonored both parties if they were not resolved in three rounds. With four rounds being exchanged and neither party withdrawing, there was only one way left to resolve the issue. On the fifth round, Thomas Geddes was shot through both thighs and Edward Simons lay dead.

John Geddes was not a man to let anything stand in his way, even if it meant sacrificing his son. John and Lavinia Fisher were nobodies. William Heyward was a repeated criminal with a long record. The three were even more insignificant.

In 1815, Juan Pablo Salas had obtained Key West in a Spanish land grant. In 1819, Spain ceded Florida to the United States. Florida was rich in prospects and attracted the interest of many individuals. With Key West now a part of the United Sates, it was destined to become a major seaport. One of those individuals interested in the Keys was the former governor of South Carolina, John Geddes.

He successfully negotiated the private purchase of Key West—or so he thought. Salas was a shrewd businessman and had sold the island to John Strong who in turn transferred his claim to Geddes. Strong had obtained the island in trade for a small sloop valued at $575. Unfortunately Salas had already sold the island to John Simonton first for $2,000. Simonton was in partnership with John Whitehead, Pardon Greene and John Fleming.

So we have the former governor of South Carolina involved in the purchase of an island in a shady scam—the very first land scam in Florida's history as part of the United States. In fact, Geddes actually took the island by force in April 1822. Geddes sent a Dr. Montgomery, George M. Geddes, two carpenters and three Negro slaves to the island with enough lumber to erect a small shed. They were assisted by Captain Hammersley of the U.S. Navy and the naval schooner *Revenge*. He obtained the island in a shady deal, seized the island by force, erected a structure and inhabited it, albeit by proxy.

Simonton and Geddes were basically in a race to file their claims. With influential friends in Washington, Simonton beat Geddes to the wire. Of course Geddes did not take the matter lying down, and it eventually took the courts to settle the matter. It was determined that Strong did not have a clear title on the sloop in question so, of course, this effected Geddes's claim. On May 23, 1828, it was ruled that John Simonton and his business partners were the legal owners of Key West.

Simonton had beat out Geddes in a shady scheme. What he gained in the matter was indeed a valuable investment. In 1822, he convinced the U.S. Navy of the value of Key West. The navy sent Lieutenant Matthew Perry to scout Key West. Perry's report was favorable, and Key West was designated a U.S. port of entry and a customs house was built. This diverted most shipping and salvaging operations away from St. Augustine. It was also closer to Cuba and a better point for their cargo.

Geddes had raced into purchasing and seizing Key West for his own benefit. If he had succeeded in obtaining Key West, he would have obtained a very valuable location ideal to shipping, trade and salvaging operations. He would have become a very rich man. Another Charlestonian, Richard Fitzpatrick, began a salvaging operation in Key West. At thirty years old, he made what would be equivalent of close to $300,000 in one year! Geddes was a salvager too, and he knew what the navy could bring to Key West for a salvager who owned the Island. The purchase of Key West also diverted shipments from St. Augustine much the same as a naval depot in Charleston would have diverted shipments from other locations. Simonton and company became very wealthy by owning the land that the U.S. Navy built its facilities on. It was what Geddes was planning and failed at achieving. Was this his plan for Charleston and the property surrounding Six Mile House? Apparently Simonton had accomplished with Key West, Florida, what Geddes had failed to do with Charleston, South Carolina. He obtained a naval depot.

We now know that all his efforts to obtain the naval base in Charleston were futile. Obviously, just like the final balloon display over Charleston as the president departed, Governor John Geddes's hopes for the naval base in Charleston went down in flames. President Monroe had the facility built in Virginia.

CHAPTER 12

Motive

THE SINS OF THE FATHER

W e now have a motive for the state's appropriation of the tracts of land containing both the Five Mile House and the Six Mile House. This gives a pretty good idea of the intended use of the land, how the state would benefit, and how the governor would definitely benefit. This also explains why the state engineer, the man directly responsible for the appropriation of land and its conversion to state use, was on the jury that indicted the owners. That explains the use of John Peoples's case and the summary judgment, but what about the David Ross case and his lynch mob seizure of the properties?

In an effort to explain that, we have to go back to the very beginning of the disputed properties.

Samuel and Joseph Wragg were brothers and the first of the Wragg family to venture to Charleston from England. They were Loyalists, loyal to the crown. Each of these brothers had a son. Samuel's son was William Wragg. Joseph's son was John Wragg.

In 1718, Samuel and his son, William, were sailing to England from Charleston. Their ship came under attack by pirates, and they were captured by none other than Blackbeard himself. They were robbed, ransomed and humiliated but otherwise released unscathed. William Wragg grew up and remained loyal to the crown. That was not a popular thing to do in revolutionary times, and he was banished from America in 1776 and his land was confiscated. He drowned off the coast of Holland on his way to England.

The same banishment happened with John Wragg, the son of Joseph Wragg. In 1758, John Wragg had inherited his father's properties. Having been banished in 1776 and having his land confiscated, there was little he could do. In 1783, he petitioned for a hearing to plead his case and have his name removed from the lists of confiscations and banishment. Apparently he was successful and received his father's land. A part of that land was in what is known as the neck area of Charleston and included a tract of land with a quarter house upon it known as Six Mile House.

John Wragg now owned the Six Mile House tract, according to the federal government, removing his disgraced father's name from the confiscations and banishment list. This was the United States doing this and not the state of South Carolina. South Carolina still views them as confiscated.

In 1796, John Wragg died leaving no heirs. In 1801, proceedings were held to have the property partitioned off and divided among his siblings and their children. A section in the city of Charleston known as Wraggsborough was also divided, and one of the relative recipients was Nathaniel Heyward. In 1810, an additional two hundred and thirteen acres belonging to the deceased John Wragg were sold to John Ball whose executors sold them to Nathaniel Heyward in 1819. Nathaniel Heyward's son was William Heyward.

There appears to now be a dispute over the property between the heirs of John Ball and Nathaniel Heyward as to who is the rightful owner.

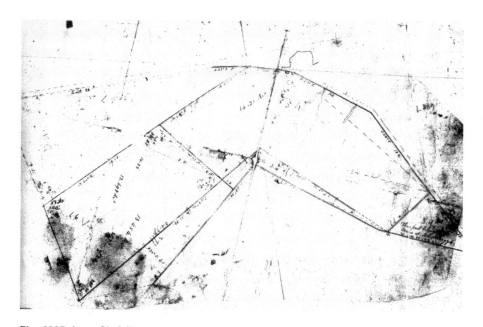

Plat 6887 shows Six Mile tract as belonging to the heirs of John Wragg. *Courtesy South Carolina Department of Archives and History.*

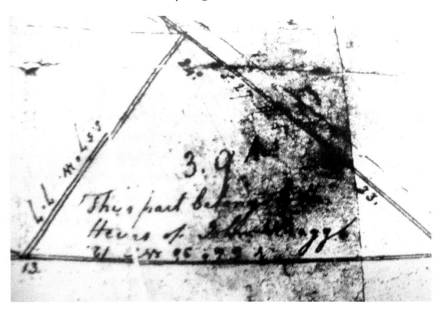

A close up of plat 6887 shows Six Mile tract as belonging to the heirs of John Wragg.
Courtesy South Carolina Department of Archives and History.

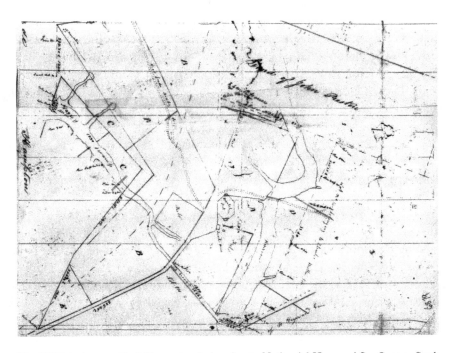

Plat 6879 designates Six Mile tract as belonging to Nathaniel Heyward Sr. *Courtesy South Carolina Department of Archives and History.*

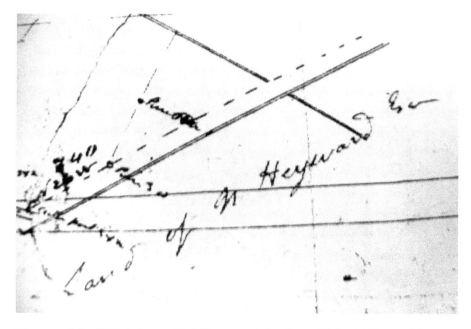

Close up of plat 6879 designates Six Mile tract as belonging to Nathaniel Heyward Sr. (upper right-hand corner). *Courtesy South Carolina Department of Archives and History.*

Remember that William Heyward was bonded out of jail by Richard Heyward and Stephen W. Moore. Stephen W. Moore would face off in court against Patrick Duncan in 1822 in a dispute two years after the execution of William Heyward. Patrick Duncan would later claim to be one of the heirs owning the Six Mile tract.

Do you remember John Wilson? He was the member of the jury in Chapter 5 that indicted Heyward and the Fishers. He was also the state engineer responsible for state improvements. Remember how it seemed strange that he would be on a jury?

From 1815, the engineer had been busy. With the end of the War of 1812, which ended in 1815, Wilson had been the surveyor of many military projects including plans for lands appropriated by the South Carolina legislature to be used for fortifications. These included lands in the neck area. By 1817, Thomas Gadsden had filed a petition asking for compensation for damage done to his property by the erection of military defenses, and John Wilson's name was included in the motions. Stephen W. Moore was also one of those parties.

In 1818, Wilson made a report on the conditions of public buildings in various districts and also on the navigability of each of the state's rivers. It is interesting

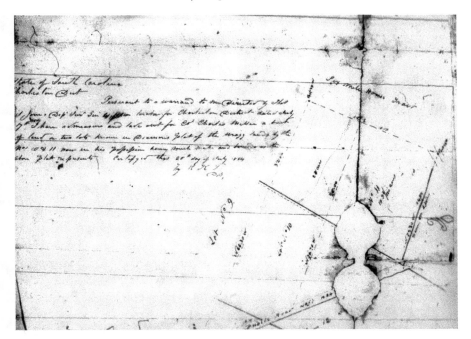

Plat 6886 shows the survey of Six Mile tract for the state of South Carolina. *Courtesy South Carolina Department of Archives and History.*

that this was done one year prior to the president's search for a location for a naval depot. Wilson had an interest in seizing lands and converting them to military use. He had obviously already been doing it in the Charleston neck area, the area that contained the Five Mile House and Six Mile House.

In 1820, the Fishers and Heyward were hanged. The sheriff, Colonel Nathaniel Greene Cleary, also was accused of framing the Fishers, and he lost the election. In 1820–1828, a judiciary committee reviewed reports made to them on the petition of the assignees and securities of N.G. Cleary asking that the amount of his contingent accounts be paid to them and not the Bank of the State to pay his debts. John Wilson was named in this action, and he signed off on the petition. This freed Cleary from paying the bank. He could settle his debts individually. This could help Cleary since the state was in a depression. Perhaps this was a trend Wilson used to help others. It also seems the state engineer, before he left office, was helping those who had helped him. In 1820, Wilson filed petition for the cancellation of his bond as civil and military engineer. No explanations and no reasons were given. Maybe he knew it was a good time to get out.

So we have the state engineer appropriating lands in the name of defense and the sheriff seizing those lands; we have the sheriff's militia clearing the property and arresting the owners; we have the state engineer sitting on the jury; we have a relative (Moore) of the accused (Heyward) involved in a dispute with the state engineer over the seizure of lands; and we have the sheriff being called out and accused publicly by the condemned and he loses reelection. He is in debt, and his creditors want to cash in. The state engineer resigns his commission. The governor goes off and tries to buy Key West, Florida, in a scam. Hmm—something does not sit well, and it appears that these three government officials were losing power in Charleston.

There is a plat dated 1795–1848 that stated 205 acres had formerly belonged to a Manigault and had been conveyed to J. Creighton, Patrick Duncan, Chisolm and Wragg. This is where Duncan staked his claim.

After receiving the property in 1819, Nathaniel Heyward had conveyed 302 acres along with 69 additional acres to his daughter Elizabeth who married Charles Manigault. The area was known as Marshfield Plantation or Manigault Farm.

Apparently the area was not successfully claimed by Patrick Duncan, and in 1880, it was sold by the descendents of the Manigaults to a Cecelia Lawton. A large portion of it became incorporated into properties belonging to the U.S. government and the navy in 1890. The Charleston Naval Clinic, formerly the Charleston Naval Hospital, now sits on the site where Six Mile House once stood. So the descendents of Heyward achieved what Geddes could not. They profited by their property going to the navy, seventy-one years after Geddes tried the same thing.

It appears that William Heyward had a right to be on the property of his father Nathaniel Heyward. If he was rightfully on his property, he had the right to defend it from seizure from the lynch mob and David Ross.

In 1813, a petition was filed by numerous persons who were assignees of the Bank of South Carolina. This petition was against William Heyward. Of the eighteen names listed, one stands out. That is the name James Fisher. James Fisher had died, and his brother, Colonel George Fisher, was the administrator of James's affairs. In 1810, he had been in a lawsuit on behalf of James against state engineer John Wilson. Wilson owed Fisher for horse gear and saddle wear. That puts George Fisher in connection with John Wilson.

James Fisher's will of August 6, 1795, is interesting. It lists his wife as Esther. It also states he had three daughters, Jane, Esther and Margaret, and one son, John. That means Colonel George Fisher is John Fisher's uncle, and James Fisher was his father.

This means that the state engineer that sat on the jury initially indicting John Fisher had a prior civil dispute with John's uncle and father. To bring things a little closer into perspective, James, the father of John Fisher, was one of the assignees in the 1813 petition against William Heyward. That puts the father of John Fisher and William Heyward also in a civil dispute. John's uncle, George Fisher, is now left with all of his responsibilities after John's father's death including his only male heir, John Fisher himself.

A plat of land in Prince William Parish near Coosawhatchee River was surveyed December 13, 1770. It lists Nathaniel Heyward and George Fisher together as owners. These are obviously related, predecessors of the other Nathaniel Heyward (owner of Six Mile) and Colonel George Fisher. The fact that they were neighbors also means they were more than likely related as property was usually divided up and willed to multiple family members.

Nathaniel Heyward had another son, other than William, named Nathaniel Heyward Jr. He died in 1819, the year before William Heyward was executed. This is the very year of the sale in which Nathaniel Heyward received the disputed land and his heirs were eliminated. One was eliminated by death and the second was incarcerated and eventually executed.

The petition against William Heyward was in the amount of $7480.00, a pretty hefty debt. A portion of that belonged to the late James Fisher. It is a debt that would have fallen on his only male heir, John. It is also a debt that Colonel George Fisher would be interested in. If he could seize an asset of William Heyward, he would have a legal foothold in securing Heyward's debt to his deceased brother.

Could the reason John Fisher was inhabiting the Six Mile House be because William Heyward had given it to him to repay the debt he owed John's father? After all, John was a living heir and entitled to repayment of the debt before his uncle, the executor, was.

Colonel George Fisher was involved in disputes with the U.S. government over land that he had prior to the Indian wars. His land was invaded in 1812 and 1813, and he had to flee. The government had moved into North Carolina to quell the Indians and restore order. He was not only trying to collect on his deceased brother's affairs in South Carolina, but he was also dealing with his own in his home state of North Carolina.

Colonel Fisher had a daughter named Anne Amelia. In 1817, she married Jack Ferrill Ross. In 1819, Jack Ferrill Ross was the first territorial state treasurer for Alabama. His wife was pregnant and would give birth to William Henrys Ross in December. Now remember the lynch mob and the first assault victim, David Ross? It is all beginning to tie in and come together now.

We now have evidence of a land and property dispute not only among various heirs of John Wragg, but also James and George Fisher, the government and the heirs. The evidence shows that William Heyward was rightfully on his father's property. With the Five Mile House and Six Mile House both belonging to Nathaniel Hayward as of 1819, the Fishers were also legitimately there. The Lynch Law seizure of the land by the mob was a pretext as most probably was the assaults on both Ross and Peoples. We now have reason and motive for the attack on Five Mile House and Six Mile House on February 18, 1819. Nathaniel Hayward had just appropriated the land—a land valuable for potential use to the military and land desired by both Colonel George Fisher and Governor Geddes. One now understands that if the Fishers had been condemned and executed for the assault on David Ross that would have given Colonel George Fisher a foothold on the land. By switching to the John Peoples case, this eliminated that foothold giving Governor Geddes and Charleston a chance at the disputed property.

It appears, from the evidence gathered, that the Fishers and Heyward were innocent in regard to where they needed to be and also in defending their property. It is strange how out of the twelve arrested for such a horrendous crime that only the owners of the properties were executed. Nine others walked away from the hangman's noose, a lot different than the legend. Remember the Toohey brothers? One was executed for murder and one received a branding in regard to the same incident. This shows that the judges in Charleston had discretion in sentencing. Peoples was beaten and robbed of between thirty five and forty dollars, and three people were executed. The Toohey brothers murdered someone, and one of them went free. The point is the charges were deliberately changed so that the three proprietors could be executed and eliminated.

Up until now there has been nothing known in regard to the lineage of either John or Lavinia Fisher. It is now known that Colonel George Fisher of North Carolina was John Fisher's uncle. This is the first connection made for him. But what is known about the lineage of Lavinia?

Lavinia has always been a dead end as far as genealogy. No one has found anything regarding who she was, who her parents were or where she came from. All anyone knew was that she was born in 1792 by simple mathematics. If she died in 1820 and was 28, then we know her date of birth. We also know that she was different than most of the fair-skinned women of Charleston. One source described her as an "Amazon or a Termagant," meaning her skin was darker.

The True Story of John and Lavinia Fisher

We also know that Lavinia believed in her innocence, and we also learned that the women of Charleston petitioned the governor to keep a white woman from hanging. They were afraid that it would set a precedent. A "decent" society would not execute a white woman for any crime; the thought of it went against any "civilized" thinking. White women were not hanged in respectable society in the mid 1800s. Why not have mercy on Lavinia and let her go? Why hang a white woman?

What if Lavinia Fisher was not considered to be white?

In an 1810 bill of sale to Dr. Joseph Glover, Colonel George Fisher's attorney, William Porter sells two slaves for the sum of $700. We know that

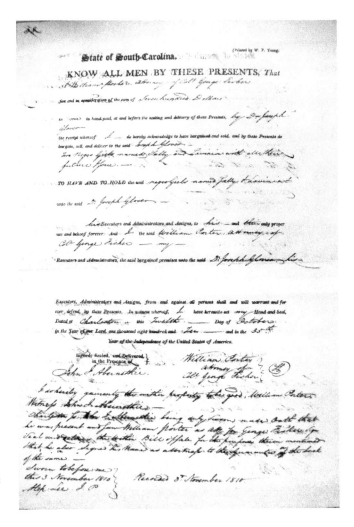

A 1810 bill of sale for two female slaves belonging to Colonel George Fisher, one of which is named Lavinia. *Courtesy South Carolina Department of Archives and History.*

An enlargement of the bill of sale. *Courtesy South Carolina Department of Archives and History.*

slaves were given the surnames of their owners for identification purposes so the obvious last name of these two would be Fisher. The bill of sale is for two young Negro girls. Their names are Sally and—Lavinia.

In 1810, Lavinia Fisher would have been eighteen, young enough to be classified as a girl. This slave would have been an eighteen year old "Lavinia Fisher." Is this a coincidence that John Fisher's uncle would have owned a slave with the same unusual name as John's future wife? The answer to that is very unlikely. What makes it even less of a coincidence is that Dr. Joseph Glover was a prominent doctor in Charleston, South Carolina. That puts a teenage slave girl by the name of Lavinia Fisher once owned by John Fisher's uncle arriving in Charleston nine years before the incident at the Six Mile House. It is an extremely giant leap to believe this is just a simple coincidence.

Suppose John had taken an interest in a slave of his uncle—not at all uncommon but not popular or accepted. What if his uncle who resided in Rowan County, North Carolina, sold her to a doctor in Charleston, South Carolina, to separate the two young teenagers? It would explain why they were ostracized and why Lavinia's lineage was unable to be traced. Could it be possible that Lavinia was a mulatto, part black and part white with very fair skin? It would explain the descriptors. It would also explain why there has been no marriage documents found. It would explain why John Fisher left North Carolina and his uncle and came back to South Carolina. It would also put a new twist in their tale: a white man in a common law marriage to a black woman in 1819.

As an added note, William Henrys Ross, the grandson of Colonel George Fisher, would marry into the Glover family—the family that bought Lavinia.

CONCLUSION

Things Are Not Always as They Appear

W e have taken actual court documents, articles, eyewitness accounts and victim statements and established that the true crimes involving John and Lavinia Fisher, William Heyward and the other persons associated with the Six Mile House crimes are quite different than what we have read and been told. As we break down the characters and events, a different story emerges that has us scratching our heads and questioning the legend.

The facts show that the incidents occurred at the Six Mile House, not the Four Mile House as many claim. The house it occurred in was burned to the ground in 1819, which was documented in the news article from that time. The Four Mile House was bulldozed in 1969.

There were no trapdoors used in Six Mile House; there was no cellar full of bodies. Dead folk have a way of turning up—literally—during construction of new buildings as you will soon read. None turned up in the area of the Six Mile House other than the two bodies (and a cow corpse), and there is no evidence they were victims.

On February 14, 1970, just four days prior to the 151st anniversary of the arrests of the Fishers at the same location, groundbreaking began for the Charleston Naval Hospital. There were no unearthed bodies and no uncovered cellars. From the time of its initial groundbreaking and its completion in 1973, nothing of the sort was recovered.

The discovery of bodies does occur periodically as you will soon learn about with the Medical University Basic Science Building's construction, but this was not the case with the hospital.

Charleston Naval Clinic (formerly Charleston Naval Hospital)—the site where Six Mile House once stood. *Courtesy of author.*

We have established that Lavinia was not a witch, a serial killer or the first female hanged in the United States. She did not use seduction or oleander tea to render her victims helpless. She may have once been a slave.

We have likewise proven that John Fisher was not a butcher or a coward. He did not shift the blame to Lavinia. In fact, he protested both her innocence, and his, right up to their executions.

The Fishers did not act alone. There were twelve named members of the gang. Ten were apprehended and four were prosecuted. Three were hanged.

No one was ever charged with murder. Lavinia Fisher was never a serial killer or a murderess. Neither is John Fisher a murderer. They were executed for highway robbery. John Peoples was the only victim that they were executed for. They were tried and convicted on assault to commit murder and common assault on David Ross, but for reasons left to speculation, this case was thrown out and the judges ruled on the Peoples case.

Lavinia was not executed separately from her husband. They were executed together at Meeting Street and the Lines. The Lines was a military barricade and fortification that the militia and citizens of Charleston constructed for defense. The location of where their execution took place would be in the vicinity of Meeting Street and Line Street today.

Lavinia was not executed in her wedding dress. According to Attorney John Blake White's eyewitness account, both of the Fishers were executed in loose white garments placed over their clothing. If Lavinia was executed in her wedding dress, John Fisher wore his wedding dress also. As a matter of fact the Six Mile House was burned to the ground immediately after their arrest. That included all of their property. Lavinia could not have sent someone to retrieve her wedding dress from Six Mile House. It would have been burned months before her execution.

Unless someone bartered for Lavinia's body after the *Charleston Courier*'s article, the bodies were buried in Charleston's potter's field. The potter's field was eventually converted to a federal arsenal in 1825. Porter Military School (eventually Porter Gaud Academy) was eventually built over the potter's field in 1880 and the Medical University of South Carolina eventually replaced Porter Military School in 1964.

During the construction of the Basic Science Building in 1968, numerous graves were unearthed. One source states that a request was made to have the bodies reinterred on James Island, but no records were found stating that actually happened. Another thirty-three graves were unearthed in 2001 with construction of the Children's Research Center. Ironically, most of these were children. They are believed to have been the victims of the yellow fever epidemic of 1819–1820. They were reinterred in March 2003 and a plaque dedicated to these deceased persons was placed near St. Luke's Church.

It reads:

> *On this site in final repose lieth the remains of thirty-three adults and children which were removed from a two hundred year old burial ground on the site of the Children's Research Building. May it serve as a solemn reminder of the suffering of an earlier time and an incentive to those who seek to eliminate diseases which afflict the children and adults of today.—March 21, 2003*

This illustrates that there is current corroborating evidence that there was a potter's field. That, accompanying the news article from 1820—"After hanging the usual time, their bodies were taken down and conveyed to Potter's Field, where they were interred"—means that Lavinia Fisher is buried somewhere beneath the MUSC Hospital and not in the Unitarian Church's cemetery as is told on the majority of ghost tours in Charleston.

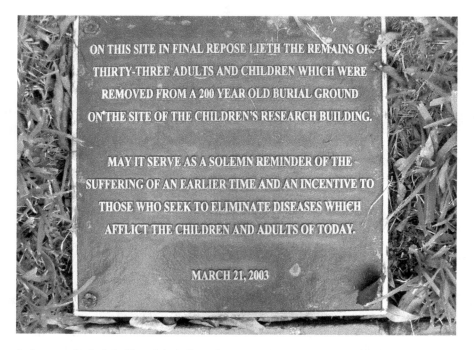

ON THIS SITE IN FINAL REPOSE LIETH THE REMAINS OF THIRTY-THREE ADULTS AND CHILDREN WHICH WERE REMOVED FROM A 200 YEAR OLD BURIAL GROUND ON THE SITE OF THE CHILDREN'S RESEARCH BUILDING.

MAY IT SERVE AS A SOLEMN REMINDER OF THE SUFFERING OF AN EARLIER TIME AND AN INCENTIVE TO THOSE WHO SEEK TO ELIMINATE DISEASES WHICH AFFLICT THE CHILDREN AND ADULTS OF TODAY.

MARCH 21, 2003

A plaque at St. Luke's Church is dedicated to unearthed bodies from Charleston's potter's field. *Courtesy of author.*

Research into this matter resulted in an official statement from the Unitarian Church to this researcher states simply, "Lavinia Fisher is not buried in our Churchyard." That is the final word on the matter. That also means that the ghost of Lavinia Fisher would have no reason to be there unless she was having a cup of tea (perhaps it was her infamous oleander tea) with the ghost of Annabel Lee, an alleged girlfriend of Edgar Allan Poe. Ironically Ms. Lee is not there either. In reality she is just a fictitious character in one of Mr. Poe's poems. Those that have seen Lavinia there or have seen her in a wedding gown anywhere have encountered a fantasy and not a phantom. This strongly lends credibility to the power of suggestion when it comes to the majority of encounters with "ghosts."

On the other hand, if there ever a person angry enough to return as a troubled spirit it would be Lavinia Fisher. You have a woman forcefully removed from her home twice, her home burned to the ground, falsely accused, imprisoned for a year, denied a pardon, her husband executed, herself executed and then—when she was finally laid to rest they build over her grave. What makes it worse is that one of the halls built over the old potter's field is named Colcock Hall. It is named after the grandson of the judge that condemned her to die in the prime of her life and deprived her of having children or grandchildren of her own. On top of that you have just about every tour guide in the city claiming she and her husband were vile murderers for the next 190 years! I think that ought to make one angry enough. If there ever were any truth to her ghost haunting the Old City Jail, she had more than enough torment in life, and in death, to keep her spirit tied to there.

Then again, her "hauntings" are the stuff of legend.

In reviewing the facts of the case, we have learned that the perpetrators were perhaps actually the victims. They were charged, prosecuted and convicted of crimes against one victim. That case was appealed and denied. They then were sentenced and executed on a completely different case, a case they never were convicted of, tried for or even charged with! No charges were ever filed involving John Peoples yet he is the reason they were hanged. The only thing that occurred in the Peoples investigation was that a statement was taken and he made identification of his assailants in an identification process that was possibly tainted, according to Fisher himself.

As G.-S. stated in his letter to his friend in Boston, "for the strongest circumstantial evidence, should be required, in a case of life and death to warrant the conviction of the accused party." There are many questions in the case that go far beyond today's standard of reasonable doubt. Unfortunately that was not something the colonial judicial system was concerned with. Their prosecutor viewed the United States Constitution and its amendments as having very little to do with colonial justice in a Charleston courtroom. As far as he and others within that judicial system were concerned, the Constitution was not worth the paper it was written on.

The Bill of Rights came into effect in the United States in 1791, twenty-eight years before the entire Six Mile incident began. The rights afforded to citizens of the United States were disregarded by Hayne and the judges in the trial of the Fishers and Heyward.

The Fourth Amendment states that:

The right of the people to be secure in their persons, houses, papers, and effects, against unreasonable searches and seizures, shall not be violated, and no Warrants shall issue, but upon probable cause, supported by Oath or affirmation, and particularly describing the place to be searched, and the persons or things to be seized.

Both Heyward and the Fishers had a right to be secure from unreasonable search and seizure. Both properties were illegally seized by a lynch mob on February 18, 1819, a mob with no warrants and no legal authority. Even though the sheriff returned the next day with a warrant to arrest the homeowners, it was because of an incident involving what would today be considered a home invasion. What makes this so incredible is that 182 years later, the attorney general of the state of South Carolina, Charlie Condon, declared an open season on home invaders. He said in an interview that, "I'm putting home invaders on notice that if an occupant chooses to use deadly force, there will be no prosecution." He declared the home as sacred ground. This is a stark contrast to his predecessor Robert Hayne.

So we have their Fourth Amendment rights violated. How about any others?

The Fifth Amendment states that "No person shall be held to answer for any capital, or otherwise infamous crime, unless on a presentment or indictment of a Grand Jury." It further states that no person shall be "deprived of life, liberty, or property, without due process of law; nor shall private property be taken for public use, without just compensation." William Heyward and the Fishers were not indicted for the crime of highway robbery against John Peoples. They were also deprived of their property without due process. It also shows that if the state was indeed interested in it, they had to compensate the owners, something the state wanted to get around. So we have their Fifth Amendment rights violated also.

The Sixth Amendment states that "In all criminal prosecutions, the accused shall enjoy the right to a speedy and public trial, by an impartial jury of the State and district where in the crime shall have been committed." They also have the right to be "confronted with the witnesses against him" and "to have compulsory process for obtaining witnesses in his favor." Neither the Fishers nor Heyward had a trial by an impartial jury or any jury at all for that matter. They never faced their accuser, Peoples, and never were allowed to present any witnesses for their defense. Their Sixth Amendment rights are violated.

The Eighth Amendment states that "Excessive bail shall not be required, nor excessive fines imposed, nor cruel and unusual punishments inflicted." The judges issued a summary judgment and sentenced them to be hanged for the crime of "Highway Robbery." This was indeed a cruel and unusual punishment in a justice system that still handed down whippings, brandings and croppings as a form of punishment.

In total there are four constitutional rights ignored by the state and denied to John and Lavinia Fisher and William Heyward. That alone should change one's view of the proceedings against the accused, but let's continue our review and delve back into the motives.

We have discovered the fact that John Fisher blamed the sheriff himself for the false accusation and for tainting the identification. This was such a strong accusation that the sheriff made an immediate rebuttal in the paper. It also may have caused him to lose reelection. We also have the state engineer, the very man responsible for converting private lands to military use for the state, sitting on the jury ensuring an indictment in the case. If you think that is interesting as far as government corruption, how about this: remember John Wragg, the original owner of the properties? He had a partnership with another merchant that was dissolved in 1749. That merchant was John Colcock. Now remember who the judge was in the—and I use the term loosely—trials? Charles Jones Colcock was the judge. The sins of the father once again descend downward through the years to the sons.

We have Colonel George Fisher trying to collect the debt of his deceased brother. We have his son-in law being a Ross and David Ross taking control of the Six Mile House in a questionable seizure under Lynch's Law. Colonel George Fisher had lost land in the Indian Wars and perhaps saw the value of the property. He may have been trying to eliminate the only heir to his brother's affairs, John Fisher. John Fisher is in the way and expendable; after all, one can speculate that he may indeed have run off with his uncle's former slave.

Colonel George Fisher claimed the property under Lynch's Law and puts David Ross over it. This is to secure his debt. Ross gets attacked and heads to town. He informs Sheriff Cleary. Ironically, two hours later, John Peoples is attacked and robbed. If you read the statement you will see that he stopped to water his horses, and the disagreement was initially over the boy with him watering the horses with a bucket. The boy refused to surrender the bucket so a conflict ensued. The watering and care of the horses at an inn was not free and was done by the keepers. It was in the keeper's right to stop the boy, so exactly who was stealing from whom?

The highway robberies were indeed occurring on the road to Charleston. Those crimes were perhaps actually committed, but were they committed by the Fishers and Heyward? They were never charged with the robberies prior to the lynch mob attack. Could the robberies in the area been a ruse to sweep the Fishers and Heyward up with the actual offenders such as Joseph Roberts and James Sterrett? We have discovered two parties reporting on a person coming forward and admitting that he was the perpetrator of the robberies, and knowing that he would be hanged, he still provided accurate details in regard to the elements of the crime. Some of these elements he may have been able to get from the newspapers, but others perhaps not. Why would a man admit to doing something others are condemned to die for? Why would John Fisher, condemned to die, admit to everything he ever did wrong in life, but deny the death penalty crime if they had truly committed the act? The answer is left to your own conclusions.

If the Fishers and Heyward were executed on the Ross case, that would justify his being there at Six Mile House and justify Colonel Fisher's claim to the property and its seizure. By having an outside party, John Peoples, leaving town and being robbed, the state would have their own "innocent" victim. By locking up John Fisher, they eliminated his claim to his father's debt against the land seized by his uncle. Colonel Fisher and the other assignees were through the state bank. By eliminating William Heyward, they eliminated the debt and the heir to the property. They paved the way to seize the property, now devoid of buildings and structures, and the state would owe no one a dime.

We have discovered that land swindles, cons, scams and seizures were not uncommon to the governor of the state of South Carolina, the governor involved in their prosecution and execution. After all he was involved in the very first land scam in Florida's history two years after the execution. We have him wanting to make Key West a naval depot; we have him diverting the president to Charleston in 1819 when President Monroe was looking for a naval depot; and we have the very lands in question eventually becoming naval property sixty years later. We know that Geddes was a salvager of wrecked vessels, which could be a $200,000- to $300,000-a-year industry for a private wrecker in Key West—a land he tried to claim. We know that the land around Six Mile House was very valuable in the fact that it could be sold to the navy and bring very valuable salvaging opportunities to the area. In fact, it eventually was sold and indeed brought a naval base, a naval shipyard and a naval hospital. To this very day, privately owned companies such as Detyen's Shipyards are still making money over that move.

The War of 1812 brought about the coastal defense system. This was the reason President Monroe was touring the South and the reason state engineer Wilson was seizing land with the governor's blessing and the sheriff's help. Even though Colonel George Fisher was the administrator of his brother James affairs, John Fisher was still the heir. John Fisher was the one who was owed the debt by William Heyward. We know that William Heyward was the son of the rightful heir to the property. By "arresting" them, seizing the property and executing them, all claims against the property would have been eliminated. Fortunately, when his son Nathaniel died in 1819 and William was arrested that same year, Nathaniel Heyward had sense enough to transfer the property to his daughter Elizabeth and her husband Charles Manigault. This kept it in the family.

The property could have been seized by the state at any time under eminent domain, but the owner would have to be compensated. Remember that the country was in its first depression and that the state had no money to spend in this endeavor. If the rightful owner was in jail, convicted of a crime and executed there would be no one to pay and the state could seize the land. There would be no one to contest the seizure and condemnation of the properties. The burning of the buildings also cleared the land of all structures. Remember that Geddes sent people to build a structure on Key West so he could claim it? Well the opposite was true. Removing the buildings also removed an element of the right to claim the property. Geddes could have the land to build the naval depot and have all the salvage rights.

It seems there is quite a different story when we come to the end of the facts. Many might say that there is a great deal of conjecture and speculation as to what did occur, but based on the facts, it is not what we have been told for the better part of two centuries. Something is greatly amiss in what happened to the Fishers.

In the end we have managed to disprove most of the legend of Six Mile House and discovered what did occur there. The only part of the legend that does ring true is the words Lavinia uttered in defiance, "Cease! I will have none of it. Save your words for others that want them. But if you have a message you want to send to Hell, give it to me; I'll carry it." That is the one true element of the legend and apparently this act of defiance— on the gallows, with her white garments blowing in the wind, denied a pardon that she begged for—was etched into the minds of the witnesses and etched into the history of Charleston. Lavinia spent her last moments in life waiting for an earthly pardon that never came and denying the godly pardon Dr. Furman and others had tried to provide her. According to legend, she is still here on earth searching for that pardon. Perhaps there is a lesson in that.

The tale of what actually did occur six miles from Charleston has now been told, and the legend of the most infamous couple in Charleston's history, John and Lavinia Fisher, has been reexamined. Based on the facts, the reader is left to draw their own conclusion as to what actually did transpire in the case of the Fishers. That conclusion is obviously quite different than what the legend has taught us and many before us over the past 190 years.

Just as the plaque outside St. Luke's Church is dedicated to those who died of disease during the same year the Fishers were arrested and executed, may this book also be a solemn reminder of the suffering of persons, like William Heyward and the Fishers, in an earlier judicial system. May it be an incentive to those who seek to investigate crimes and render justice today to not be swayed by bias, politics or by prejudice. May it also serve as a reminder that not everything you are told is true and that the truth is often overshadowed by time and lost in legend.

BIBLIOGRAPHY

Ashley, Clifford W. *The Ashley Book of Knots*. New York: Double Day, 1944.

Browne, Jefferson B. *Key West: The Old and the New St. Augustine, Fla.* St. Augustine, FL: Record Company Printers and Publishers, 1912.

Bulloch, J.G.B. MD. *The Lineage Book of the Order of Washington*. New York: Astor, Lennox and Tilden Foundations, 1916.

Buxton, Geordie, and Ed Macy. *Haunted Charleston: Stories from the College of Charleston, the Citadel, and the Holy City*. Charleston, SC: The History Press, 2004.

Charleston (SC) Courier, January 1819–December 1820.

Charleston (SC) Evening Post, October 14, 1969.

Coverly, Nathaniel. *Some Particulars Relative to John and Lavinia Fisher, His Wife Who Were Executed at Charleston, SC Feb. 18, 1820 to Which are Added Remarks on Crime and Punishment, With Other Miscellaneous Observations*. Boston: privately printed, 1820.

Cutler, H.G., and Yates Snowden. *History of South Carolina*. Vol. 5. Chicago and New York: Lewis Publishing Company, 1920.

"Ghosts of the Lowcountry." *Southern Haunts*, DVD. Directed by Zac Adams. Nashville, TN: Skydive Films/Harpeth Productions, 2007.

Gulf States Historical Magazine 1 (July 1902–May 1903).

Hendrix, Pat. *Murder and Mayhem in the Holy City*. Charleston, SC: The History Press, 2006.

Jervy, Theodore. *Robert Y. Hayne and His Times*. New York: Da Capo Press, 1970.

John Blake White Papers, 1800–1844. (1116.00) South Carolina Historical Society, Charleston, SC.

Jones, Jack. "Condon Calls for 'Open Season' on Home Invaders." *Spartanburg Herald Journal,* January 25, 2001.

Jones, Mark R. *Wicked Charleston: The Dark Side of the Holy City.* Charleston, SC: The History Press, 2005.

Leland, Isabella Gaud. *Charleston, Crossroads of History: a Story of the South Carolina Low Country.* Sun Valley, CA: American Historical Press, 1980.

Maiken, Peter T., and Terry Sullivan. *Killer Clown: The John Wayne Gacy Murders.* New York: Pinnacle Books/Windsor Publishing Company, 2000.

Manley, Roger. *Weird Carolinas.* New York: Sterling Publishing, 2007.

Martin, Margaret Rhett. *Charleston Ghosts.* Columbia: University of South Carolina Press, 1963.

Miller, Tom. *The Copeland Killings: The Bizarre True Account of Ray and Faye Copeland, The Oldest Couple Ever Sentenced to Death in America.* New York: Pinnacle Books/Windsor Publishing Company, 1993.

News and Courier (Charleston, SC). December 8, 1932; February 18, 1940; and October 14, 1969.

Patterson, Lane. "The Battle of Giants: Webster and Hayne: Orators at Odds." *American History Illustrated* 17 (February 1983): 18–23.

Preservation Progress 12, no. 2 (March 1967).

Ravenel, Beatrice St. Julien. *Architects of Charleston.* Columbia: University of South Carolina Press, 1992.

———, ed. *Charleston Murders.* New York: Duell, Sloan and Pierce, 1947.

Rogers, George C. *Charleston in the Age of the Pinckneys.* Norman: University of Oklahoma Press, 1969.

Rogers, James A. *Richard Furman Life and Legacy.* Macon, GA: Mercer University Press, 1985.

South Carolina Historical and Genealogical Magazine 19 (January 1918–January 1919).

Thoms, Herbert. "Early Obstetrics in America." *Yale Journal of Biology and Medicine* 4, no. 5 (May 1932).

The Twentieth Century Biographical Dictionary of Notable Americans. Vol. 9. Boston: Biographical Society, 1904.

Wallace, David Duncan. *South Carolina: A Short History.* Chapel Hill: University of North Carolina Press, 1969.

Ward, Bernie. *Families Who Kill.* New York: Pinnacle Books/Windsor Publishing Company, 1993.

White, Coyte W. "Lavinia Fisher—One Hell of a Hostess," *Lowcountry News and Reviews* [Charleston, SC], September 13–27, 1977.

Whitehead, Charles. *The Autobiography of Jack Ketch*. Philadelphia: Carey, Lea and Blanchard, 1835.

Wikipedia. "Hanging," http://en.wikipedia.org/w/index.php?title=Hanging&oldid=306327846 (accessed August 6, 2009).

———. "James Monroe." http://en.wikipedia.org/w/index.php?title=James_Monroe&oldid=306654803 (accessed August 7, 2009).

———."John Geddes." http://en.wikipedia.org/w/index.php?title=John_Geddes&oldid=294984052 (accessed June 7, 2009).

———. "Key West, Florida." http://en.wikipedia.org/w/index.php?title=Key_West,_Florida&oldid=306507656 (accessed August 7, 2009).

———. "Panic of 1819." http://en.wikipedia.org/w/index.php?title=Panic_of_1819&oldid=297247255 (accessed June 18, 2009).

———. "Robert Y. Hayne." http://en.wikipedia.org/w/index.php?title=Robert_Y._Hayne&oldid=303298716 (accessed July 21, 2009).

———. "William Lynch (Lynch Law)." http://en.wikipedia.org/w/index.php?title=William_Lynch_(Lynch_law)&oldid=298487926 (accessed June 25, 2009).

ABOUT THE AUTHOR

Bruce Orr was raised in the Lowcountry of South Carolina and grew up hunting and fishing the plantations of Berkeley County with his father and brothers. It was during those times he spent many evenings listening to the tales and legends surrounding this historic area. As a young boy, he had an insatiable appetite for the bizarre, unexplained and paranormal and was always searching for answers behind the events he heard at the hunt clubs and fish camps.

Courtesy of Kayla Orr.

As he grew into an adult, this natural curiosity in seeking the facts brought him into law enforcement where he eventually became a detective and a supervisor within his agency's Criminal Investigative Division. Now retired, he uses the skills he obtained in his career to research some of the most notorious cases within the Charleston area. He seeks answers through historical documentation in an effort to separate fact from fantasy and to keep the truth from being lost in legend.

Printed in the USA
CPSIA information can be obtained
at www.ICGtesting.com
LVHW021913101123
763593LV00001B/1